CONTENTS

INTERVENTION

During their occupation by Germany in World War II, France had to surrender control of its territory in Indochina to Japan in 1941. In Vietnam, Japan's only enemies were the Viet Minh nationalists led by leader Ho Chi Minh.

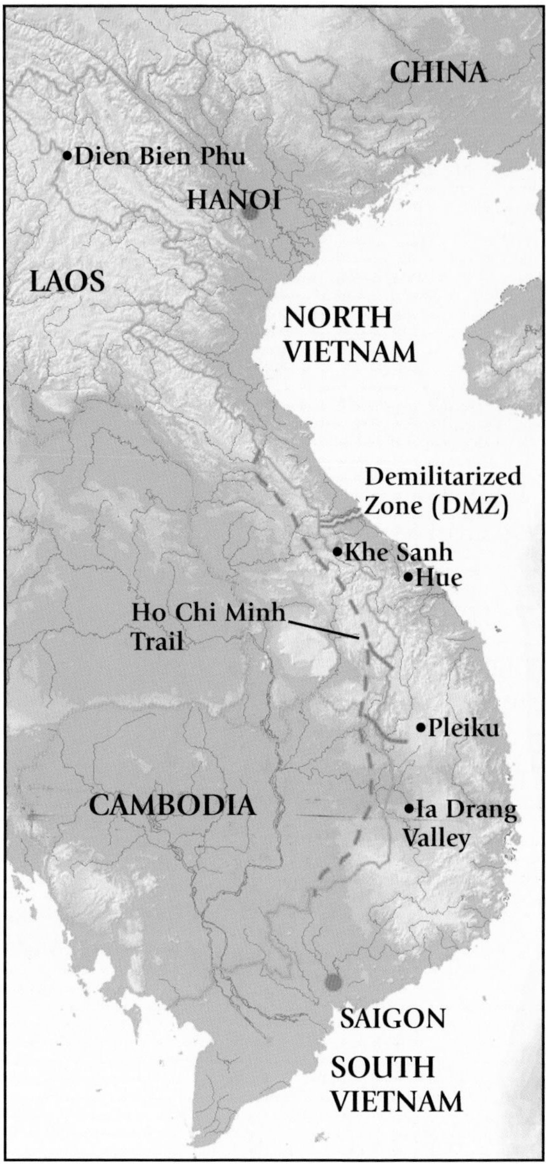
CHINA
•Dien Bien Phu
HANOI
LAOS
NORTH
VIETNAM
Demilitarized
Zone (DMZ)
•Khe Sanh
•Hue
Ho Chi Minh
Trail
•Pleiku
CAMBODIA
•Ia Drang
Valley
SAIGON
SOUTH
VIETNAM

Part of the peninsula formerly known as Indochina, Vietnam was divided into the Democratic Republic of Vietnam to the north and the Republic of Vietnam to the south in 1954.

The French War

Partly aided by the Allies, the Viet Minh resisted the Japanese. At the end of World War II, they declared independence.

Meanwhile the Allies had decided Vietnam should be returned to French control. The Viet Minh were ejected from Hanoi in 1946. Aided by newly communist China, the Viet Minh rebelled in 1949, starting a war.

The conflict in Korea had ushered in the Cold War era—a competition between the United States and the Soviet Union for control or influence over other countries. Now, the Viet Minh were viewed as a communist threat to Southeast Asia.

The United States provided arms to the French, but the Viet Minh, armed by the Soviets, were stronger. The fighting raged until an assault at Dien Bien Phu ended in a decisive French defeat.

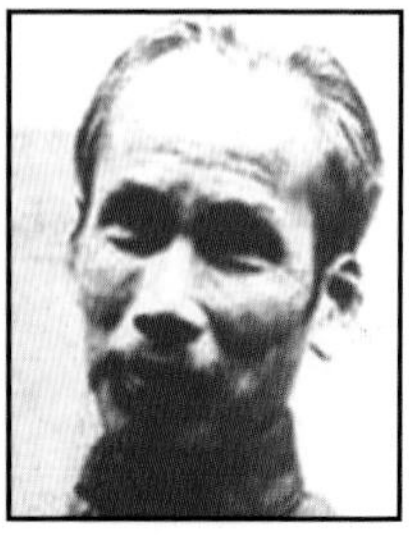

Charismatic leader Ho Chi Minh warned the French, "You will kill ten of our men and we will kill one of yours, yet in the end it is you who will tire."

GRAPH ▮▮▮▮▮▮▮▮ HISTORY:
COLD WAR CONFLICTS

THE VIETNAM
WAR

By Gary Jeffrey & Illustrated by Nick Spender

Crabtree Publishing Company
www.crabtreebooks.com

Crabtree Publishing Company
www.crabtreebooks.com
1-800-387-7650

Publishing in Canada
616 Welland Ave.
St. Catharines, ON
L2M 5V6

Published in the United States
PMB 59051, 350 Fifth Ave.
59th Floor,
New York, NY

Published in **2014 by CRABTREE PUBLISHING COMPANY.**

Printed in Hong Kong/092013/BK20130703

Created and produced by:
David West Children's Books

Project development, design, and concept:
David West Children's Books

Author and designer: Gary Jeffrey
Illustrator: Nick Spender
Editors: Lynn Peppas, Kathy Middleton
Proofreader: Kelly McNiven
Project coordinator: Kathy Middleton
Production coordinator and Prepress technician: Ken Wright
Print coordinator: Margaret Amy Salter
Photographs: p6b, U.S. Air Force; p7t, p7m, p44m, p46, NARA; p7b, Office of the Deputy Chief of Staff for Operations. U.S. Army Audiovisual Center; p45t, USAF

Library and Archives Canada Cataloguing in Publication

Jeffrey, Gary, author
The Vietnam War / by Gary Jeffrey and illustrated by Nick Spender.

(Graphic modern history : Cold War conflicts)
Includes index.
Issued in print and electronic formats.
ISBN 978-0-7787-1236-7 (bound).--ISBN 978-0-7787-1240-4 (pbk.).--ISBN 978-1-4271-9347-6 (pdf).--ISBN 978-1-4271-9343-8 (html).--

1. Vietnam War, 1961-1975--Juvenile literature. 2. Vietnam War, 1961-1975--Comic books, strips, etc. 3. Graphic novels. I. Spender, Nik, illustrator II. Title. III. Series: Jeffrey, Gary. Graphic modern history. Cold War conflicts

DS557.72.J45 2013 j959.704'3 C2013-904135-4
C2013-904136-2

Library of Congress Cataloging-in-Publication Data

Jeffrey, Gary, author.
The Vietnam War / by Gary Jeffrey and illustrated by Nick Spender.
pages cm -- (Graphic modern history: Cold War conflicts)
Includes index.
ISBN 978-0-7787-1236-7 (reinforced library binding) -- ISBN 978-0-7787-1240-4 (pbk.) -- ISBN 978-1-4271-9347-6 (electronic pdf) -- ISBN 978-1-4271-9343-8 (electronic html)
1. Vietnam War, 1961-1975--Campaigns--Juvenile literature. 2. Vietnam War, 1961-1975--Campaigns--Comic books, strips, etc. I. Spender, Nik, illustrator. II. Title.

DS557.7.J45 2013
959.704'3--dc23

Men trapped at Dien Bien Phu dug in to try to survive the fierce Viet Minh attack. A few weeks later, in May 1954, the French agreed to leave Vietnam. France's attempt to keep Indochina had cost them 90,000 troops.

ATTACKED FROM WITHIN

Elections to unite Vietnam under one leadership were cast aside as the United States took over funding the repressive and unpopular government of the South. In 1959, the communist National Liberation Front (NLF) was formed in the North to wage a guerrilla war on the South. By 1964, the NLF, also known as the Viet Cong, had grown to 100,000 members.

The American government feared the "domino theory" of communism—if one country fell to communism, so might the countries surrounding it.

F-105s dropped bombs on the targets of Rolling Thunder.

A ROLLING GIANT

The United States decided South Vietnam could not be allowed to fall to the communists. In February 1965, U.S. forces launched Operation Rolling Thunder—a continuous bombing campaign of military targets in North Vietnam.

The following month, the first combat troops arrived to protect U.S. air bases from attack. While the Viet Cong got stronger, the South Vietnamese army (ARVN) destabilized as generals staged coups and counter coups. In July, the United States announced a deployment of 100,000 troops to South Vietnam.

ESCALATION

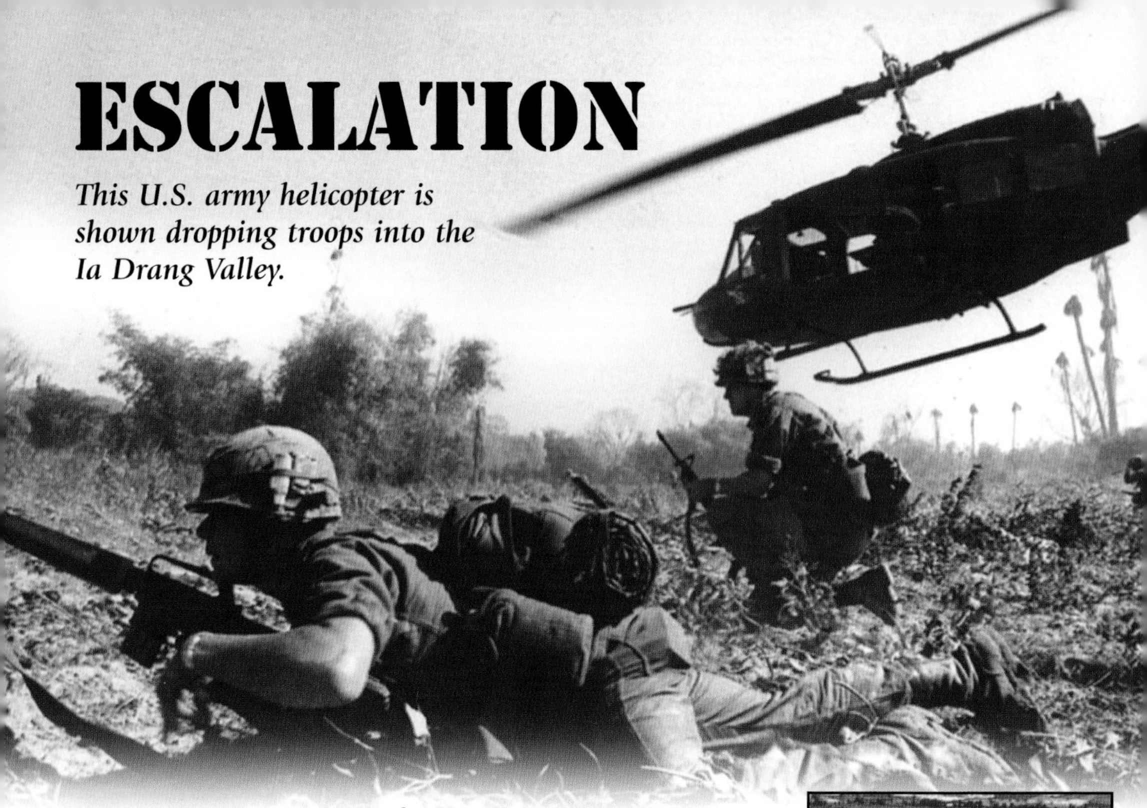

This U.S. army helicopter is shown dropping troops into the Ia Drang Valley.

The powerful United States was facing off against a poor, third world country ravaged by decades of war. But it could only fight a limited war. If U.S. actions brought other countries into the war, it might result in World War III.

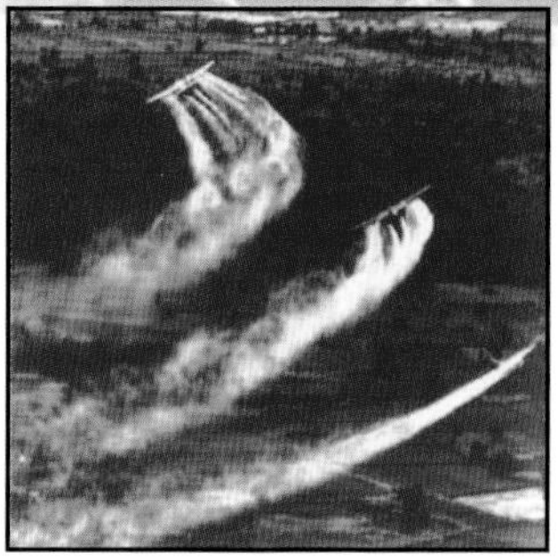

Agent Orange was used to kill jungle plants hiding the Viet Cong.

Military Solutions

U.S. General William Westmoreland's strategy was to wipe out the Viet Cong using search-and-destroy tactics rather than taking and holding ground. In the fierce Battle of Ia Drang Valley in November of 1965, 3,561 North Vietnamese Army (NVA) soldiers were killed compared with 305 American soldiers. The North Vietnamese commander Vo Nguyen Giap used guerrilla tactics. Viet Cong units would get in close when attacking American targets to avoid artillery or air strikes, then vanish over the Cambodian border. Throughout 1966 and 1967, U.S. forces operated countless helicopter, land, and river missions to ambush Viet Cong units and destroy their supply routes and staging areas.

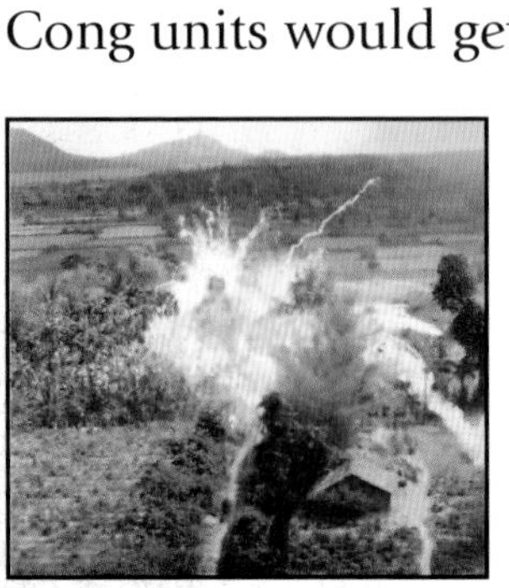

A napalm bomb engulfs a straw hut suspected of housing Viet Cong.

TURNING POINT

By December 1967 the number of American forces in Vietnam had reached 500,000. On January 21, 1968, the American marine base at Khe Sanh came under heavy attack by the NVA. It was a diversion ahead of a surprise mass assault by 84,000 Viet Cong on multiple targets across the South. It would take place during the lunar New Year holiday, called Tet, even though both sides had agreed to a two-day cease-fire. Viet Cong forces had been decimated, and this was the last chance for Ho Chi Minh and Giap.

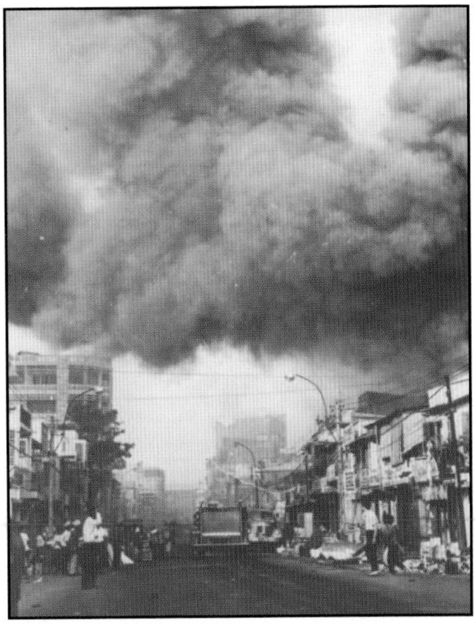

The sky over Saigon was heavy with smoke during the Tet assault.

Just before the attack, Westmoreland's claimed victory was close at hand. Then, fighting erupted around American bases and in Saigon, even breaking through the gates of the U.S. Embassy. Although the Viet Cong were defeated with appalling losses, the television coverage alarmed the American public.

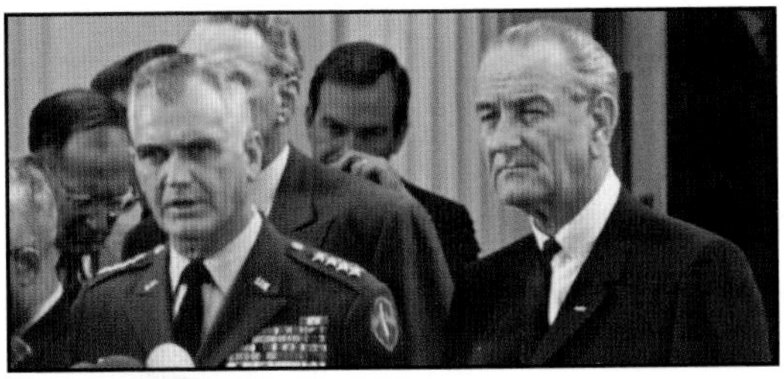

The Tet Offensive damaged the credibility of both Westmoreland and the U.S. government.

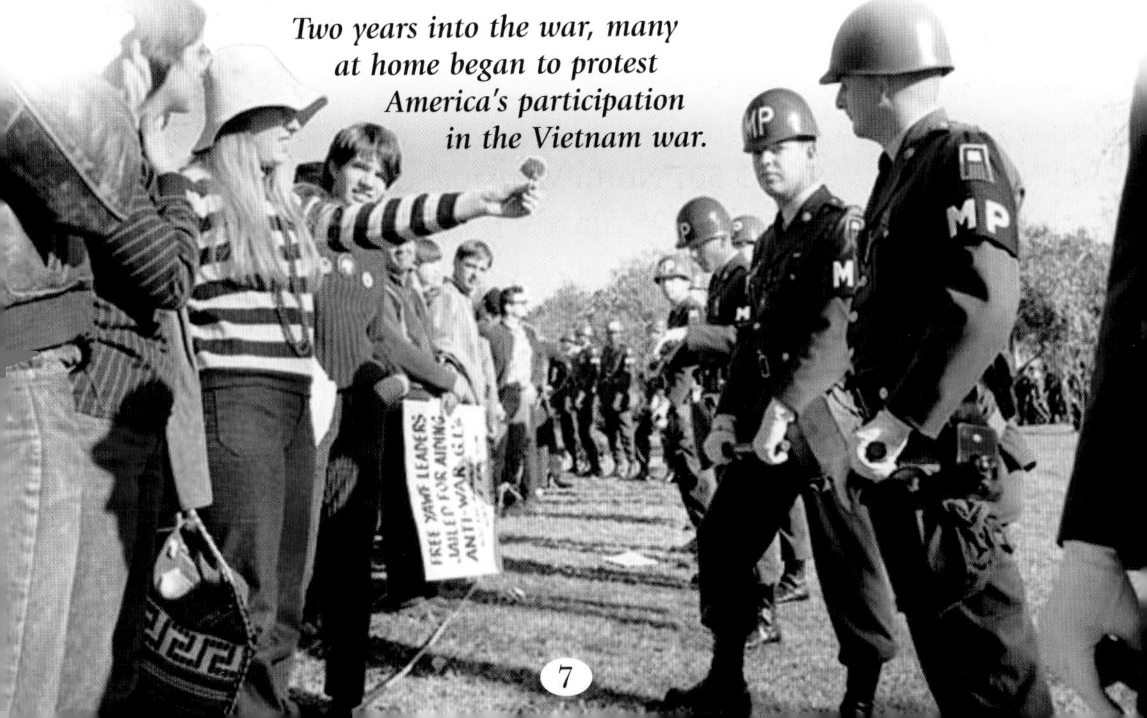
MP
MP

Two years into the war, many at home began to protest America's participation in the Vietnam war.

RESCUE AT LZ ALBANY

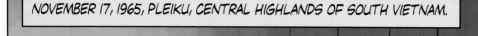

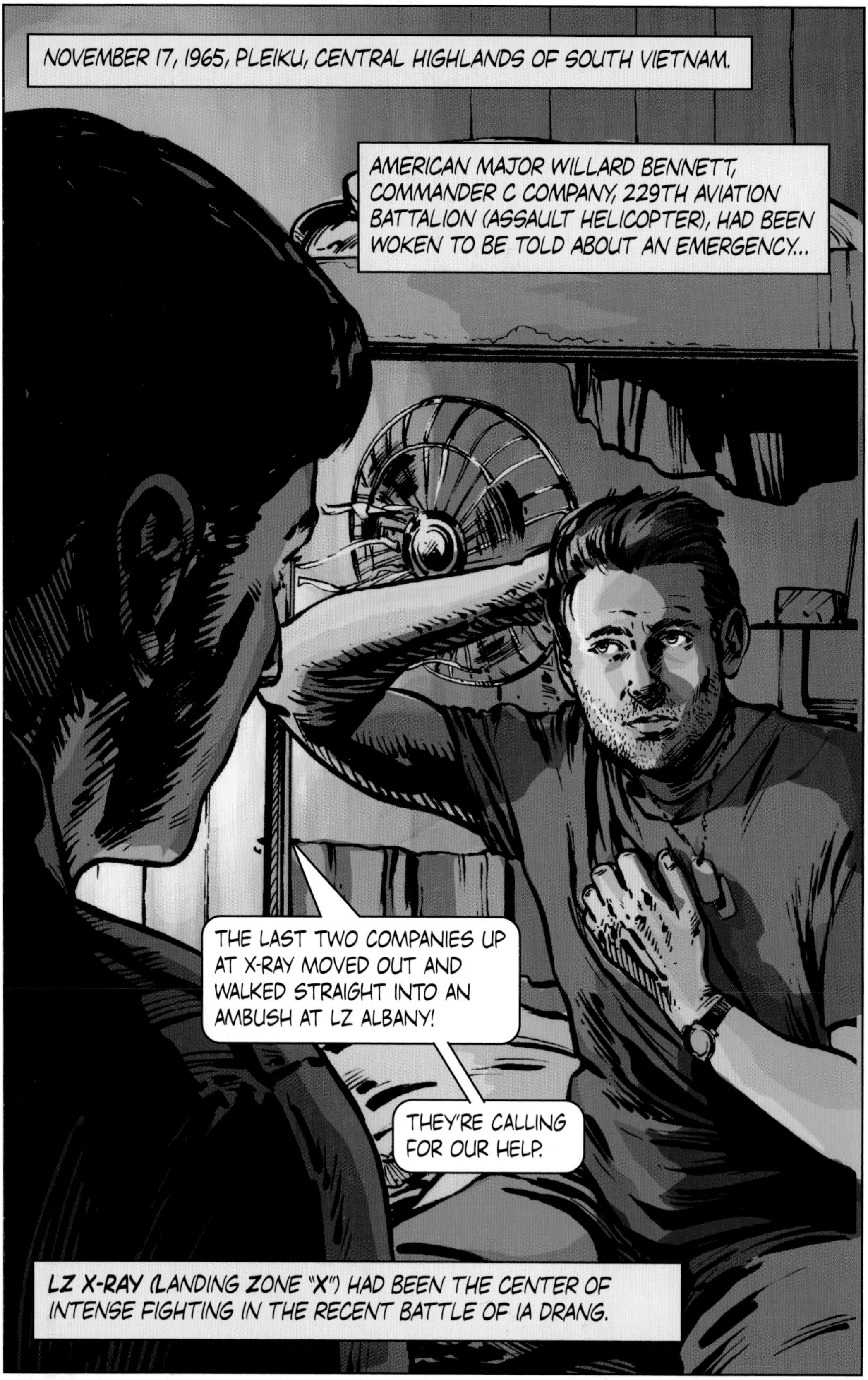

NOVEMBER 17, 1965, PLEIKU, CENTRAL HIGHLANDS OF SOUTH VIETNAM.

AMERICAN MAJOR WILLARD BENNETT, COMMANDER C COMPANY, 229TH AVIATION BATTALION (ASSAULT HELICOPTER), HAD BEEN WOKEN TO BE TOLD ABOUT AN EMERGENCY...

THE LAST TWO COMPANIES UP AT X-RAY MOVED OUT AND WALKED STRAIGHT INTO AN AMBUSH AT LZ ALBANY!

THEY'RE CALLING FOR OUR HELP.

LZ X-RAY (LANDING ZONE "X") HAD BEEN THE CENTER OF INTENSE FIGHTING IN THE RECENT BATTLE OF IA DRANG.

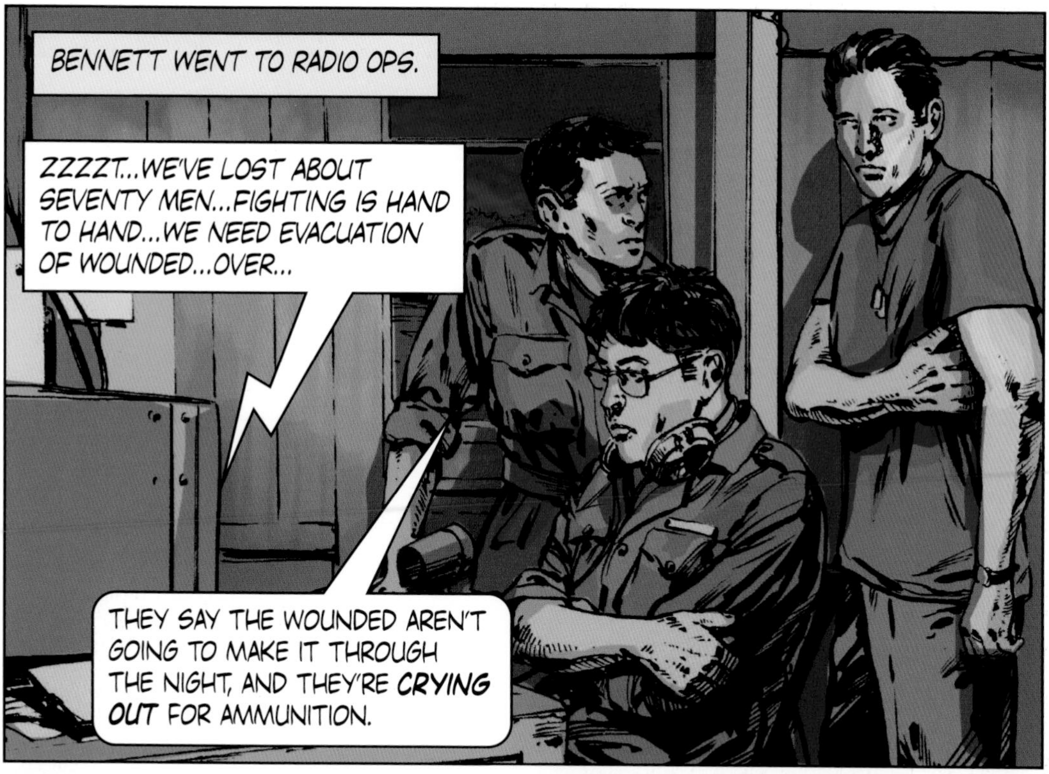
BENNETT WENT TO RADIO OPS.
ZZZZT...WE'VE LOST ABOUT SEVENTY MEN...FIGHTING IS HAND TO HAND...WE NEED EVACUATION OF WOUNDED...OVER...
THEY SAY THE WOUNDED AREN'T GOING TO MAKE IT THROUGH THE NIGHT, AND THEY'RE CRYING OUT FOR AMMUNITION.

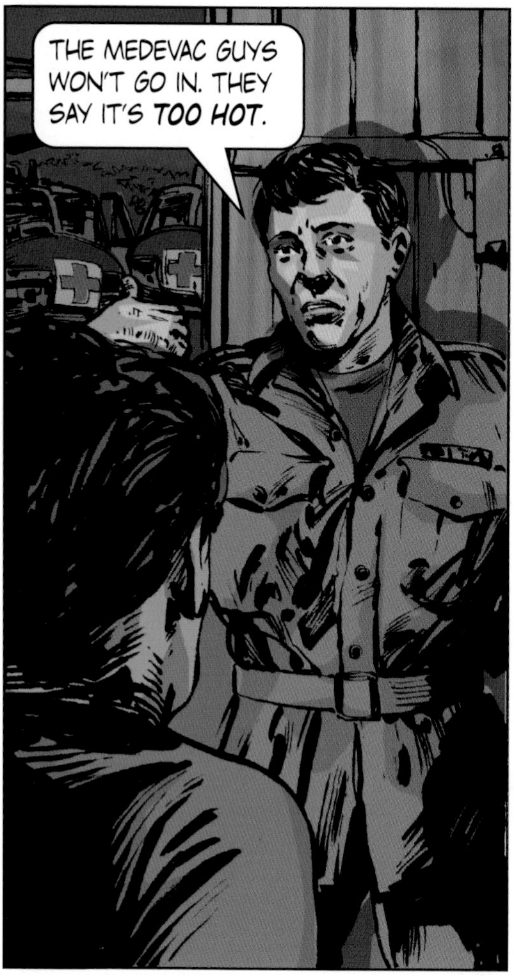
THE MEDEVAC GUYS WON'T GO IN. THEY SAY IT'S TOO HOT.

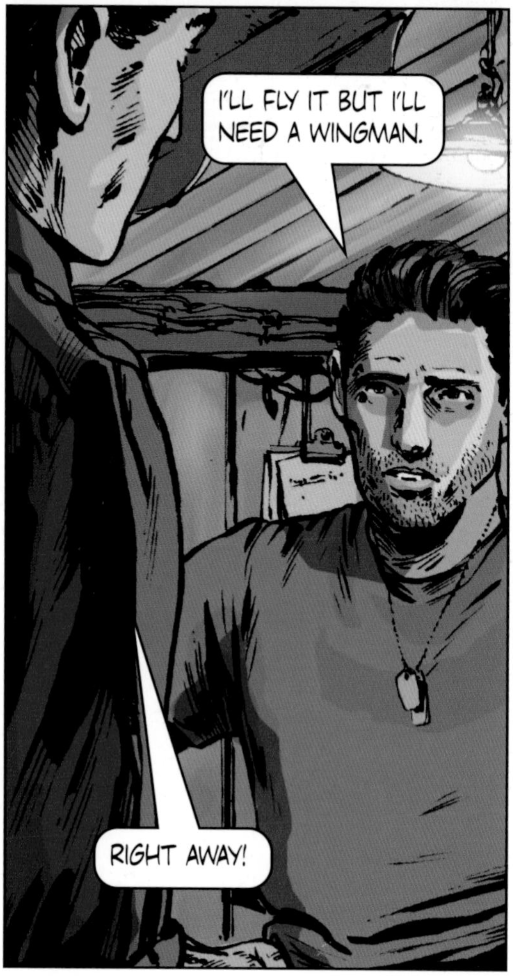
I'LL FLY IT BUT I'LL NEED A WINGMAN.
RIGHT AWAY!

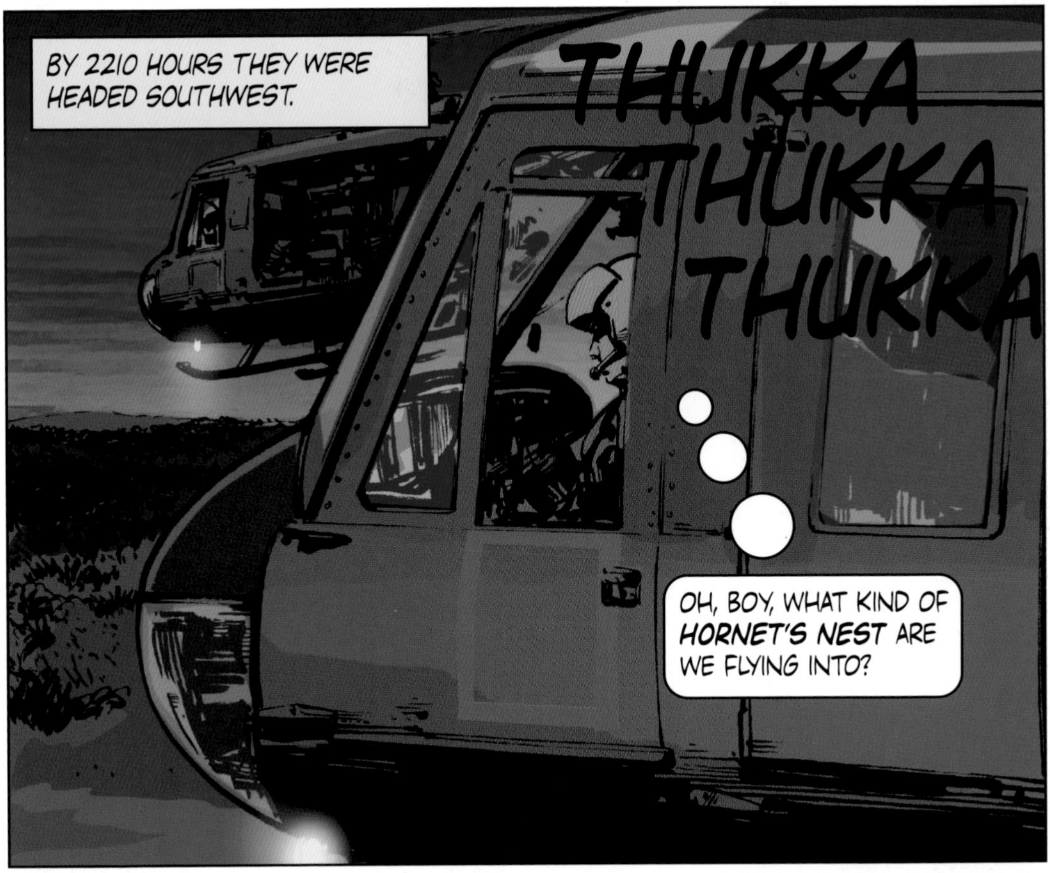
BY 2210 HOURS THEY WERE HEADED SOUTHWEST.
THUKKA THUKKA THUKKA
OH, BOY, WHAT KIND OF **HORNET'S NEST** ARE WE FLYING INTO?

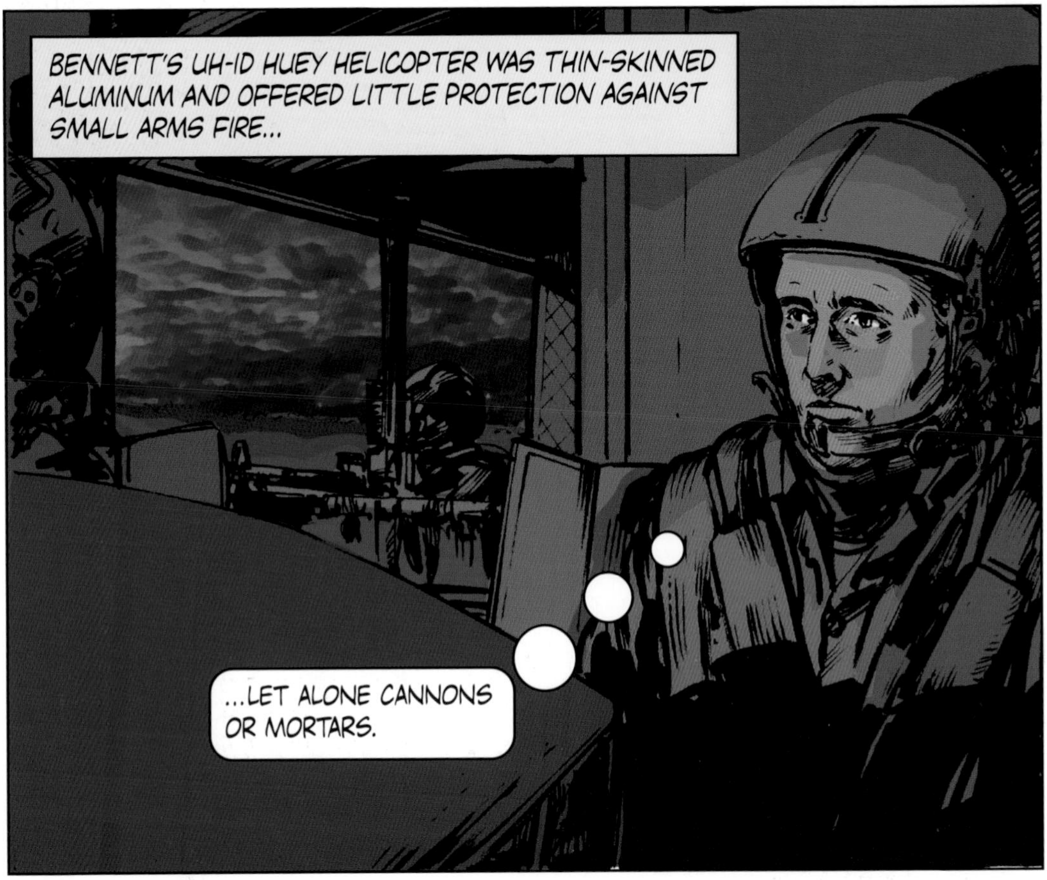
BENNETT'S UH-1D HUEY HELICOPTER WAS THIN-SKINNED ALUMINUM AND OFFERED LITTLE PROTECTION AGAINST SMALL ARMS FIRE...
...LET ALONE CANNONS OR MORTARS.

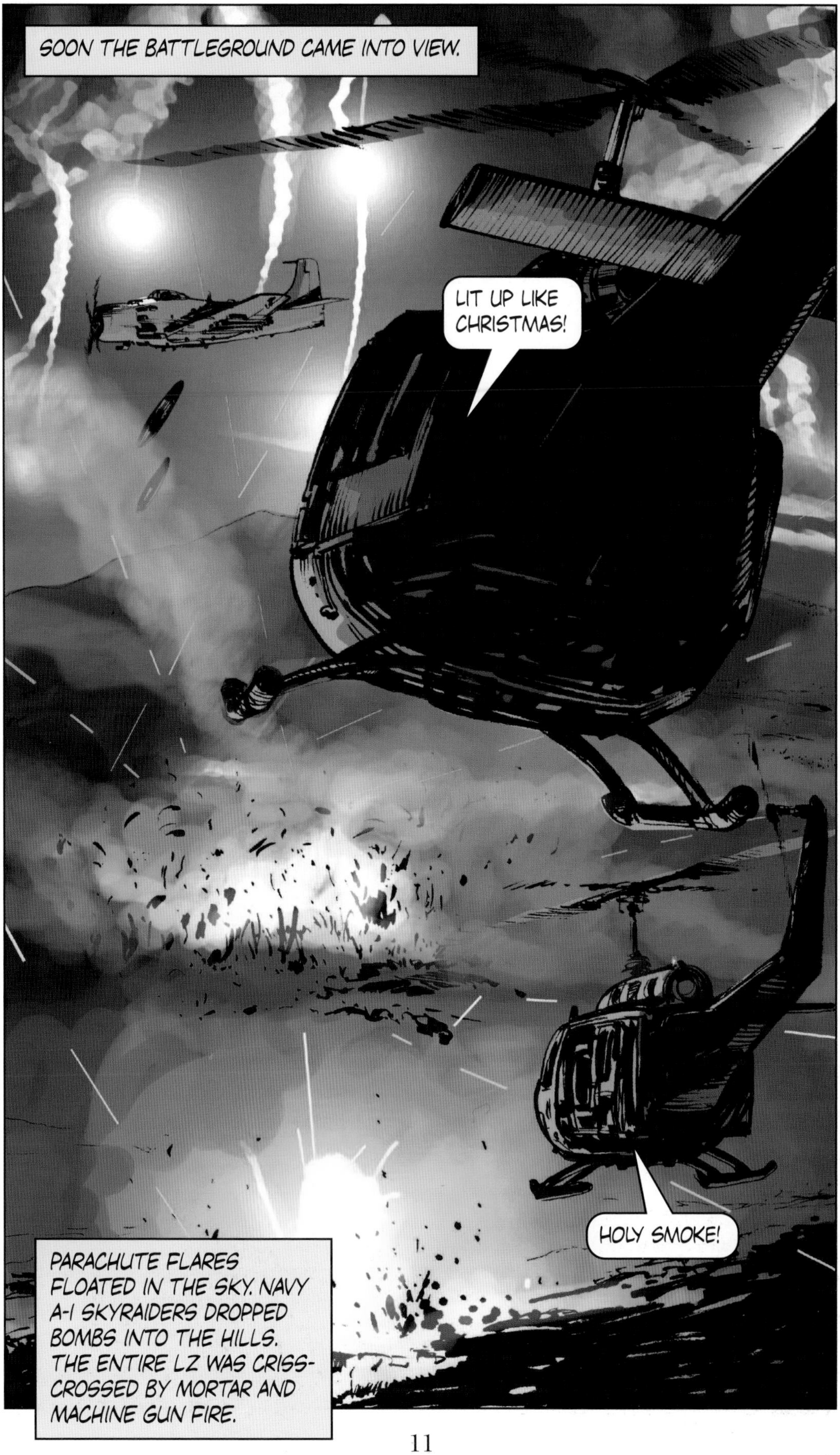
SOON THE BATTLEGROUND CAME INTO VIEW.
LIT UP LIKE CHRISTMAS!
HOLY SMOKE!
PARACHUTE FLARES FLOATED IN THE SKY. NAVY A-1 SKYRAIDERS DROPPED BOMBS INTO THE HILLS. THE ENTIRE LZ WAS CRISS-CROSSED BY MORTAR AND MACHINE GUN FIRE.

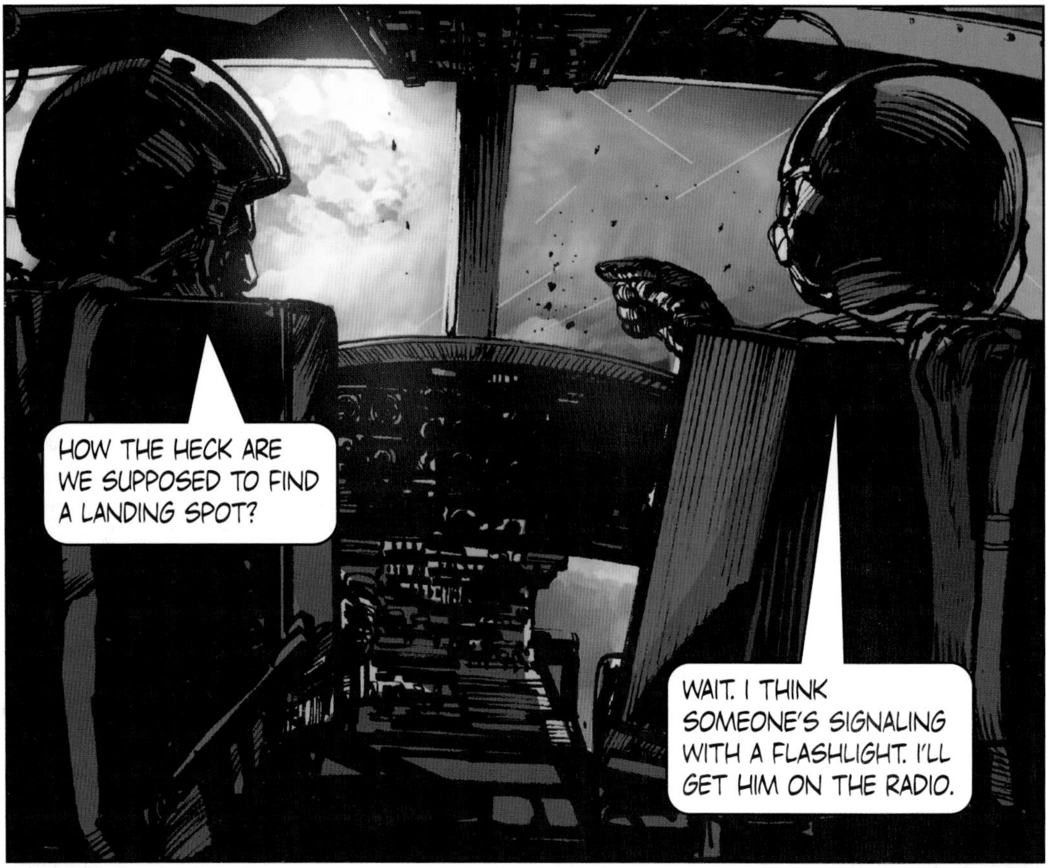
HOW THE HECK ARE WE SUPPOSED TO FIND A LANDING SPOT?
WAIT. I THINK SOMEONE'S SIGNALING WITH A FLASHLIGHT. I'LL GET HIM ON THE RADIO.

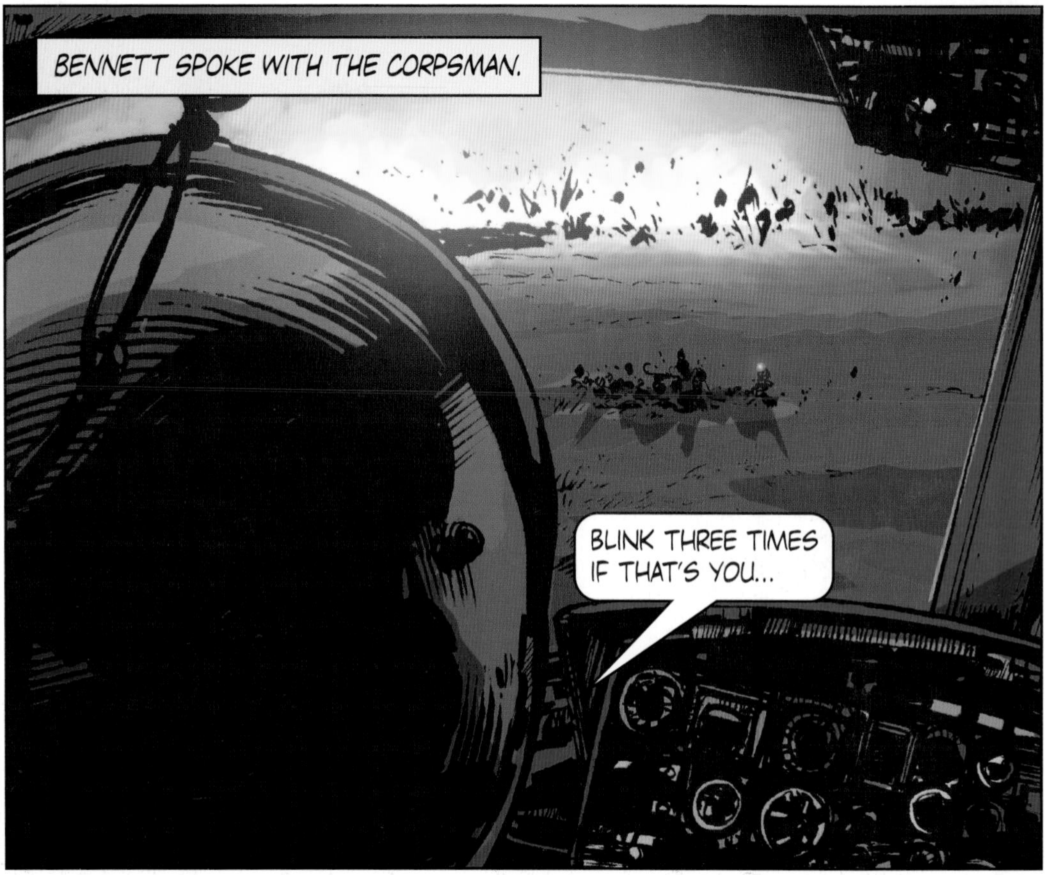
BENNETT SPOKE WITH THE CORPSMAN.
BLINK THREE TIMES IF THAT'S YOU...

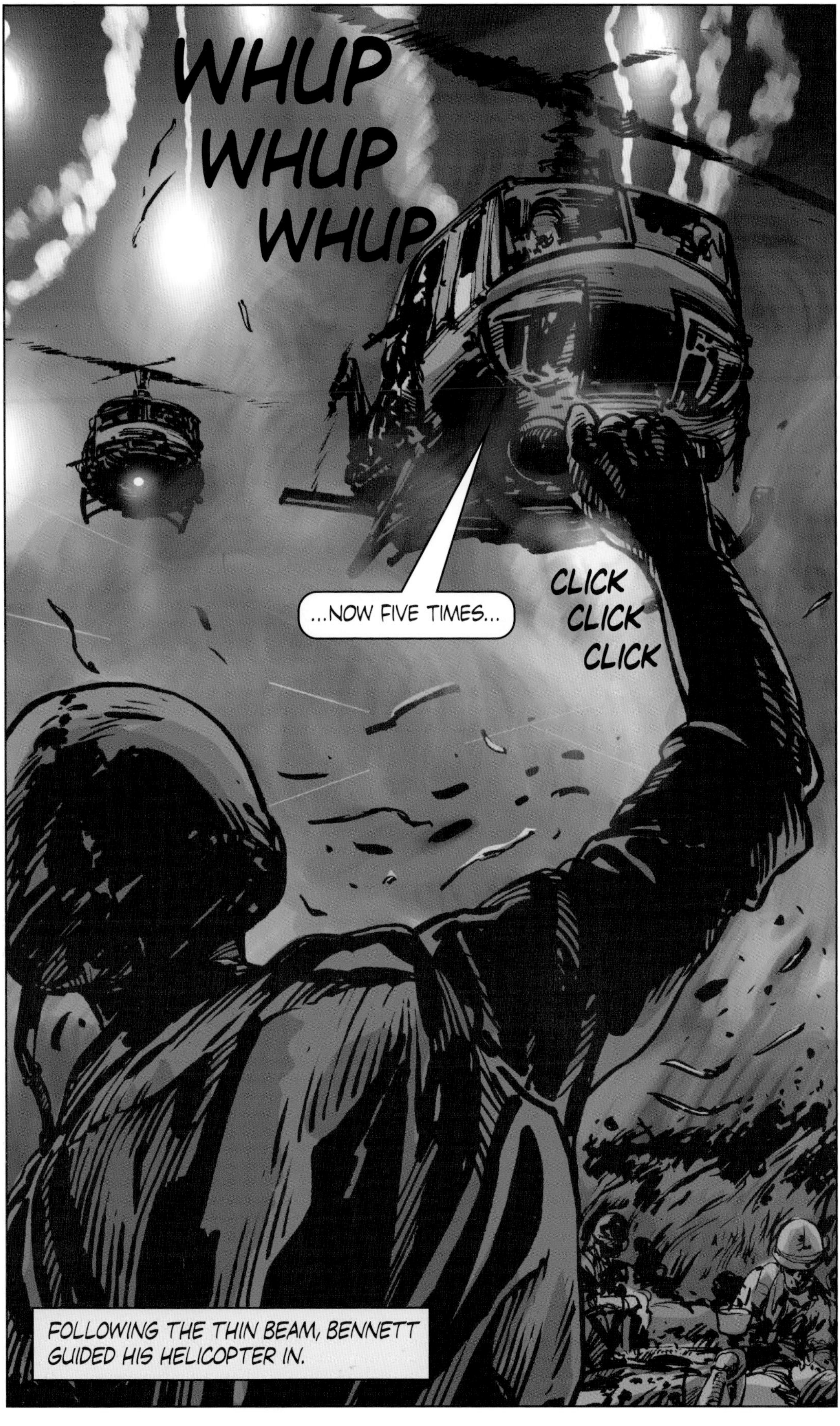
WHUP
WHUP
WHUP
...NOW FIVE TIMES...
CLICK
CLICK
CLICK
FOLLOWING THE THIN BEAM, BENNETT GUIDED HIS HELICOPTER IN.

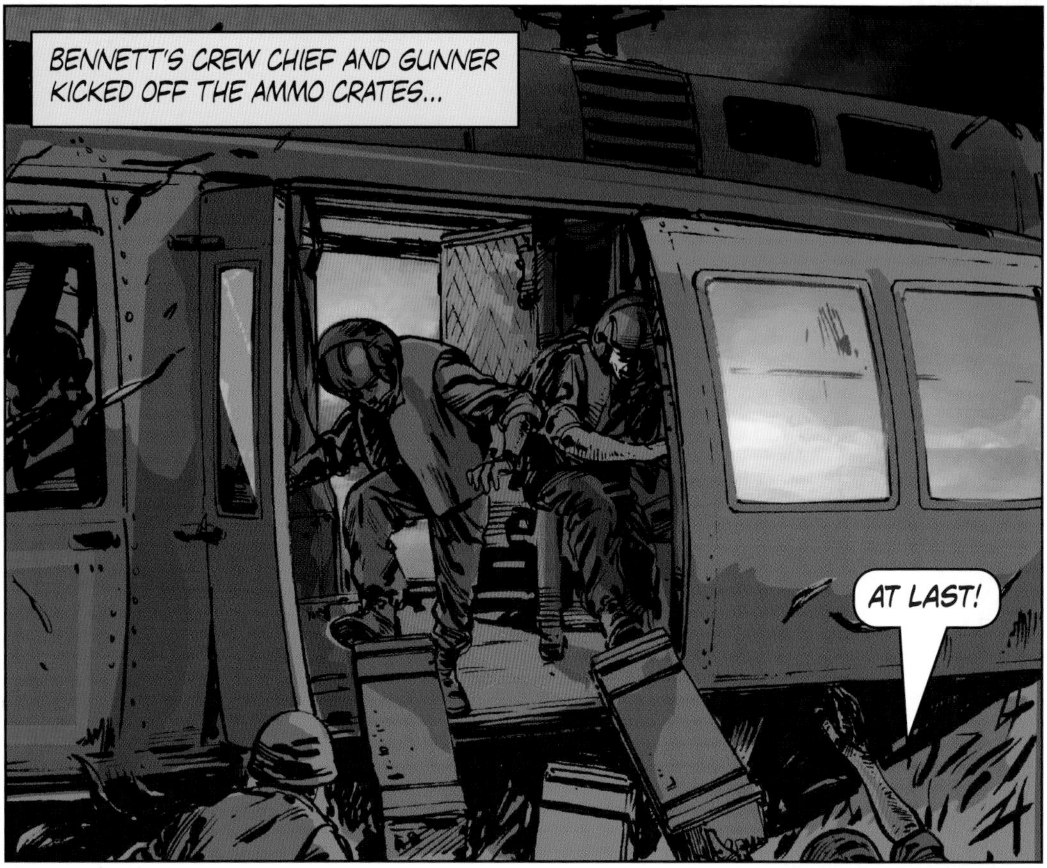
BENNETT'S CREW CHIEF AND GUNNER KICKED OFF THE AMMO CRATES...
AT LAST!

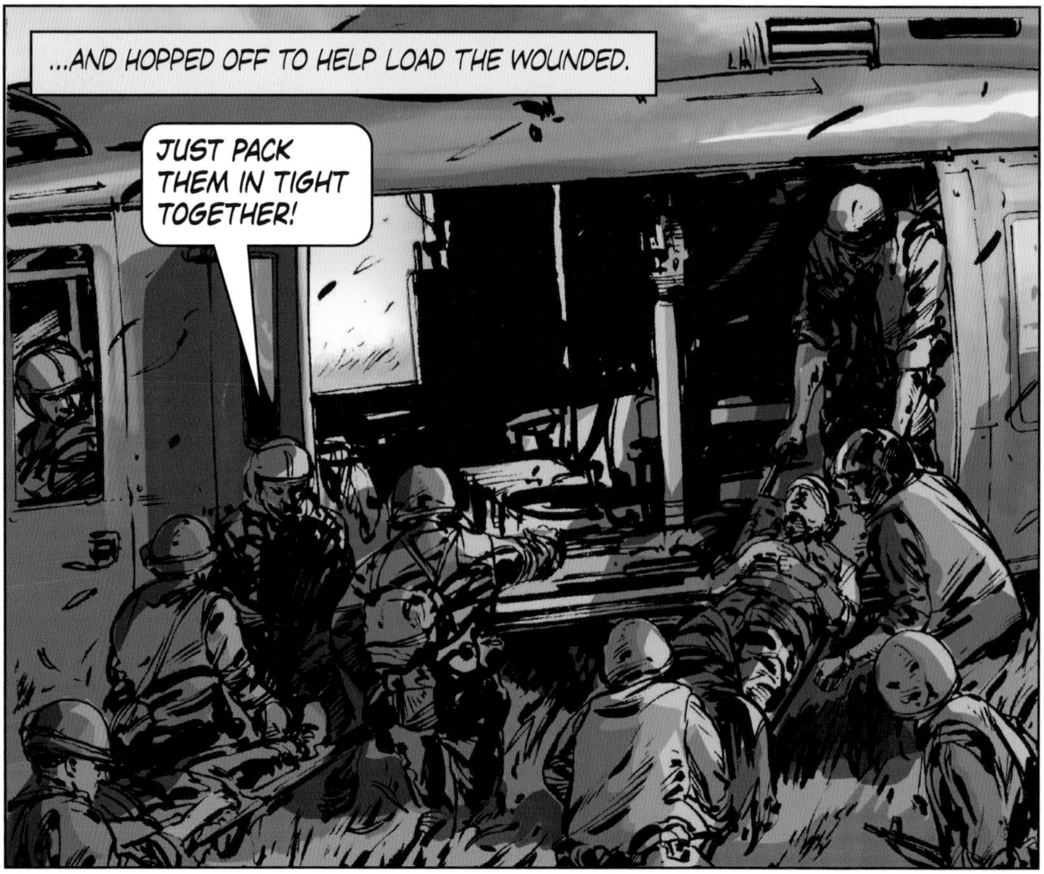
...AND HOPPED OFF TO HELP LOAD THE WOUNDED.
JUST PACK THEM IN TIGHT TOGETHER!

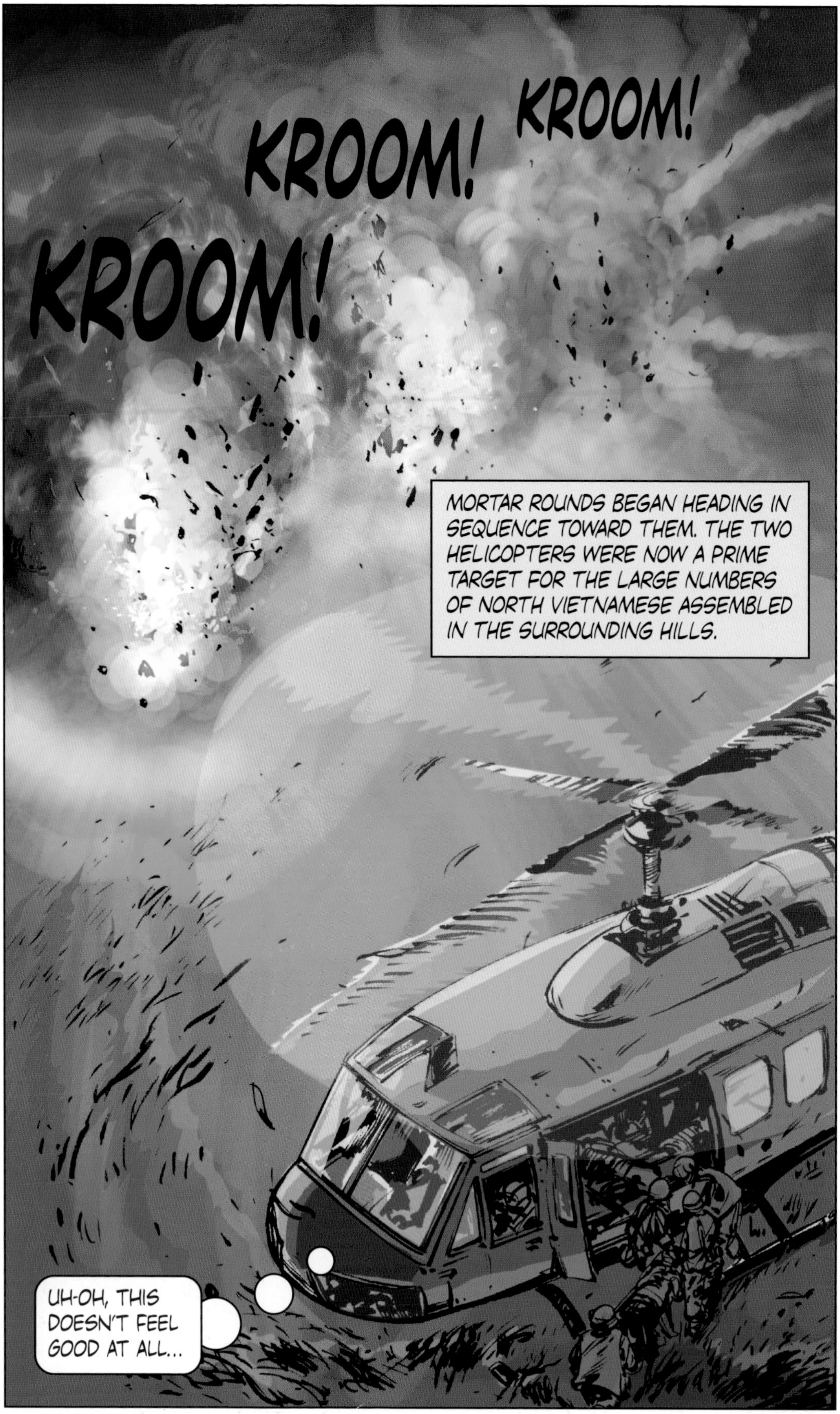
KROOM!
KROOM!
KROOM!
MORTAR ROUNDS BEGAN HEADING IN SEQUENCE TOWARD THEM. THE TWO HELICOPTERS WERE NOW A PRIME TARGET FOR THE LARGE NUMBERS OF NORTH VIETNAMESE ASSEMBLED IN THE SURROUNDING HILLS.
UH-OH, THIS DOESN'T FEEL GOOD AT ALL...

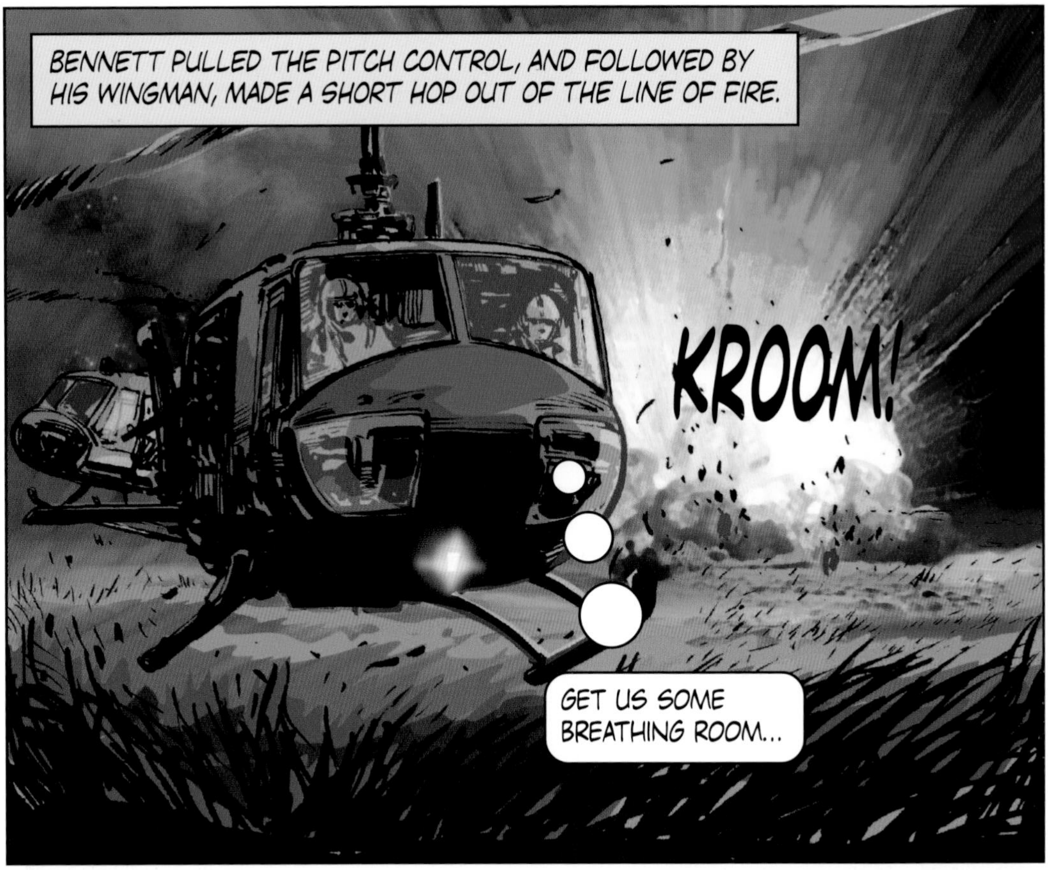
BENNETT PULLED THE PITCH CONTROL, AND FOLLOWED BY HIS WINGMAN, MADE A SHORT HOP OUT OF THE LINE OF FIRE.
KROOM!
GET US SOME BREATHING ROOM...

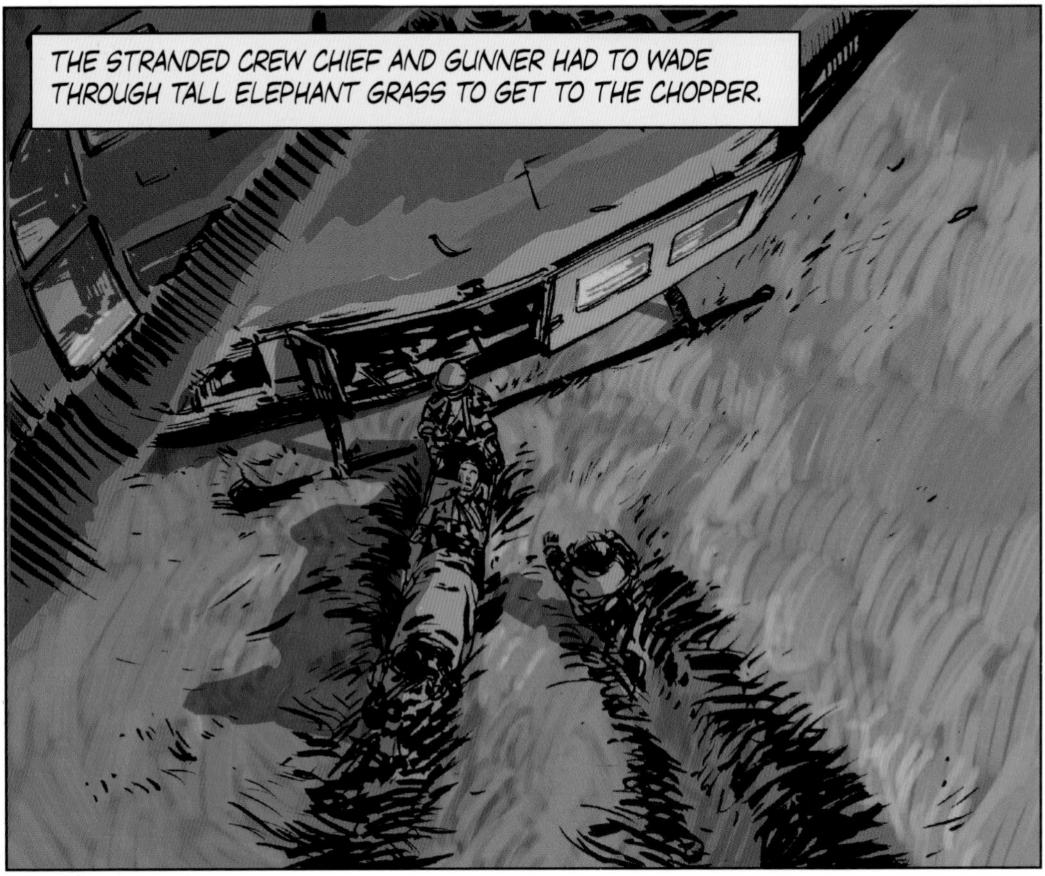
THE STRANDED CREW CHIEF AND GUNNER HAD TO WADE THROUGH TALL ELEPHANT GRASS TO GET TO THE CHOPPER.

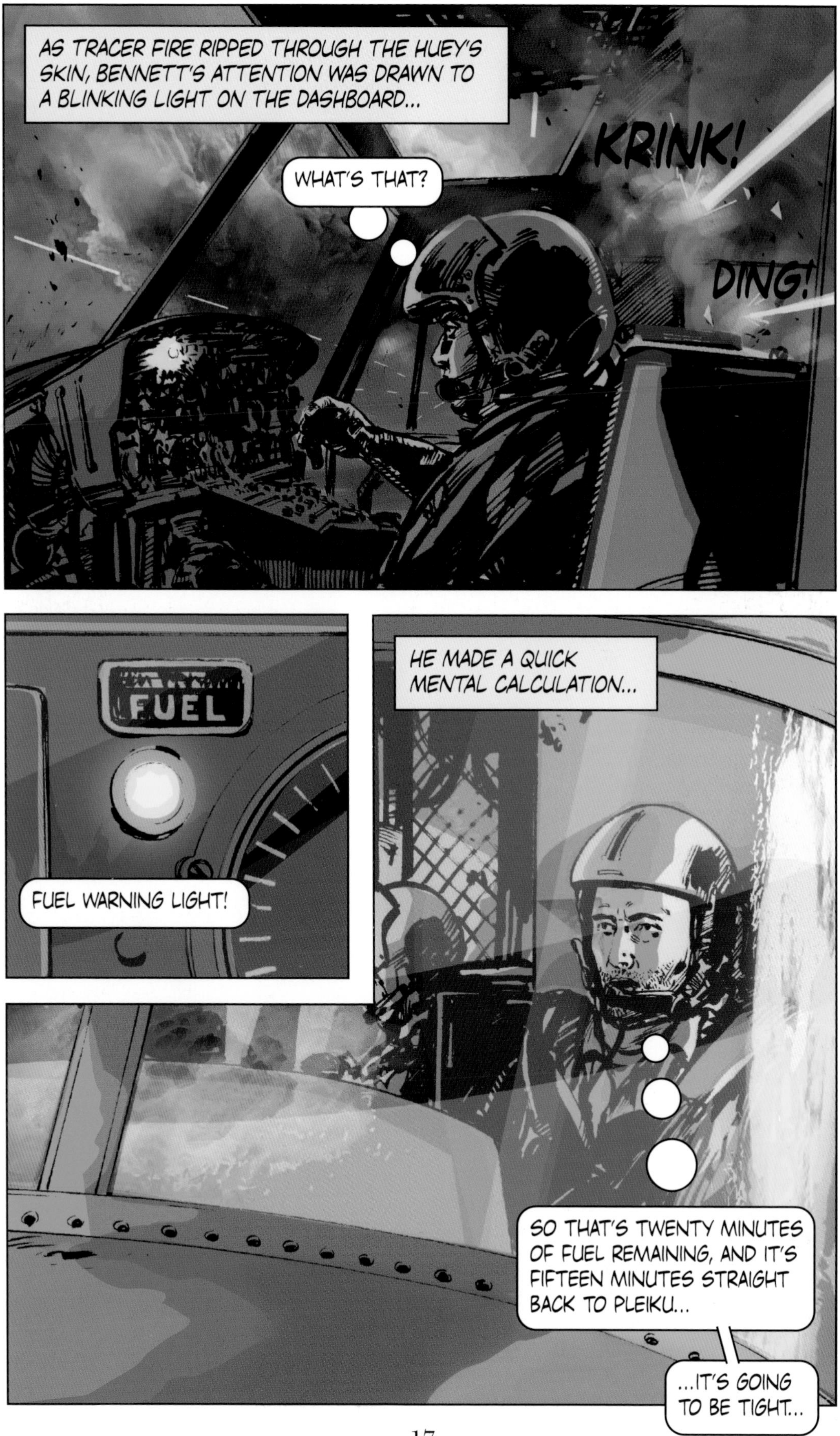

AS TRACER FIRE RIPPED THROUGH THE HUEY'S SKIN, BENNETT'S ATTENTION WAS DRAWN TO A BLINKING LIGHT ON THE DASHBOARD...
WHAT'S THAT?
KRINK!
DING!
FUEL
FUEL WARNING LIGHT!
HE MADE A QUICK MENTAL CALCULATION...
SO THAT'S TWENTY MINUTES OF FUEL REMAINING, AND IT'S FIFTEEN MINUTES STRAIGHT BACK TO PLEIKU...
...IT'S GOING TO BE TIGHT...

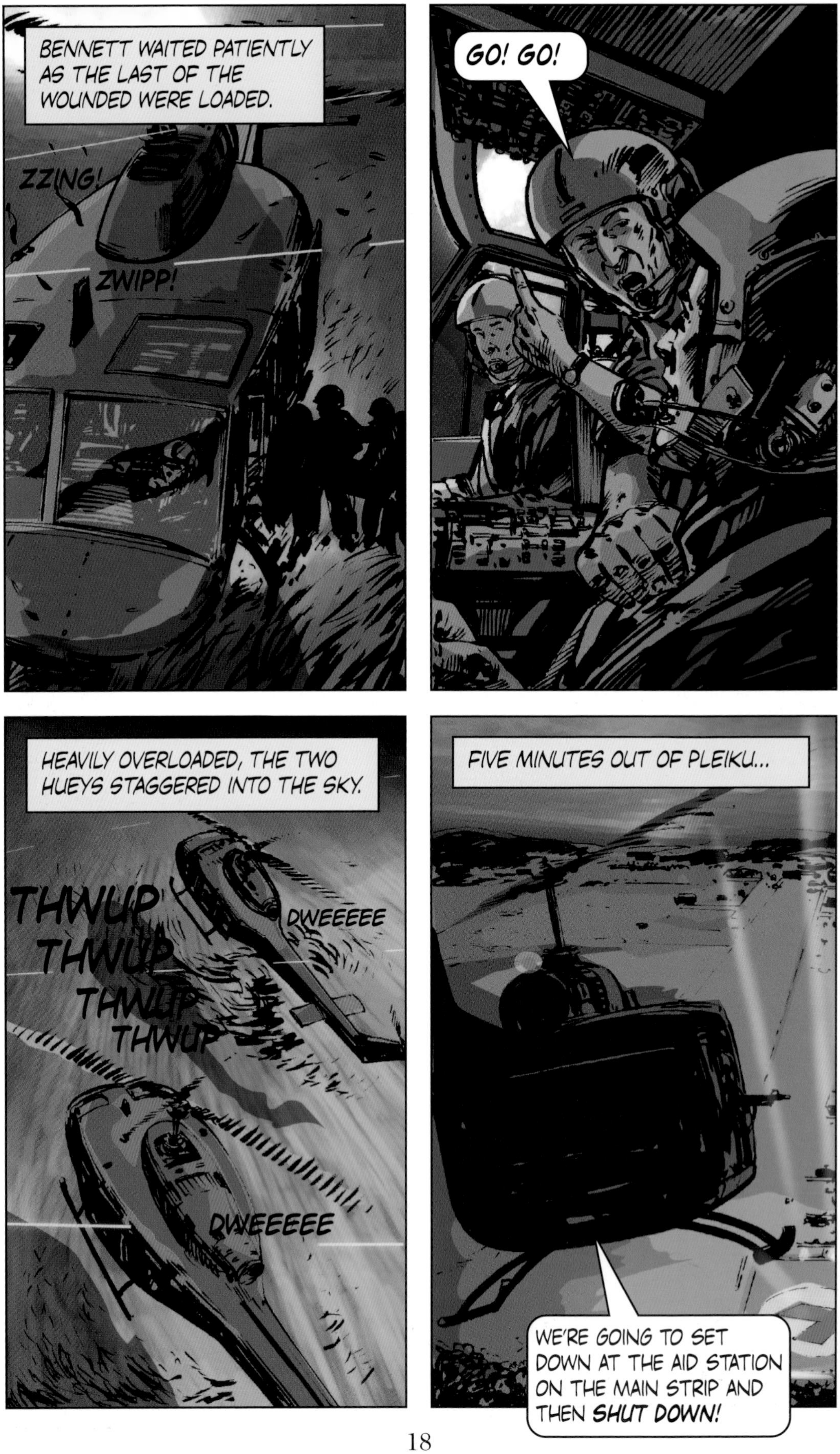
BENNETT WAITED PATIENTLY AS THE LAST OF THE WOUNDED WERE LOADED.
ZZING!
ZWIPP!
GO! GO!
HEAVILY OVERLOADED, THE TWO HUEYS STAGGERED INTO THE SKY.
THWUP THWUP THWUP THWUP
DWEEEEE
DWEEEEE
FIVE MINUTES OUT OF PLEIKU...
WE'RE GOING TO SET DOWN AT THE AID STATION ON THE MAIN STRIP AND THEN SHUT DOWN!

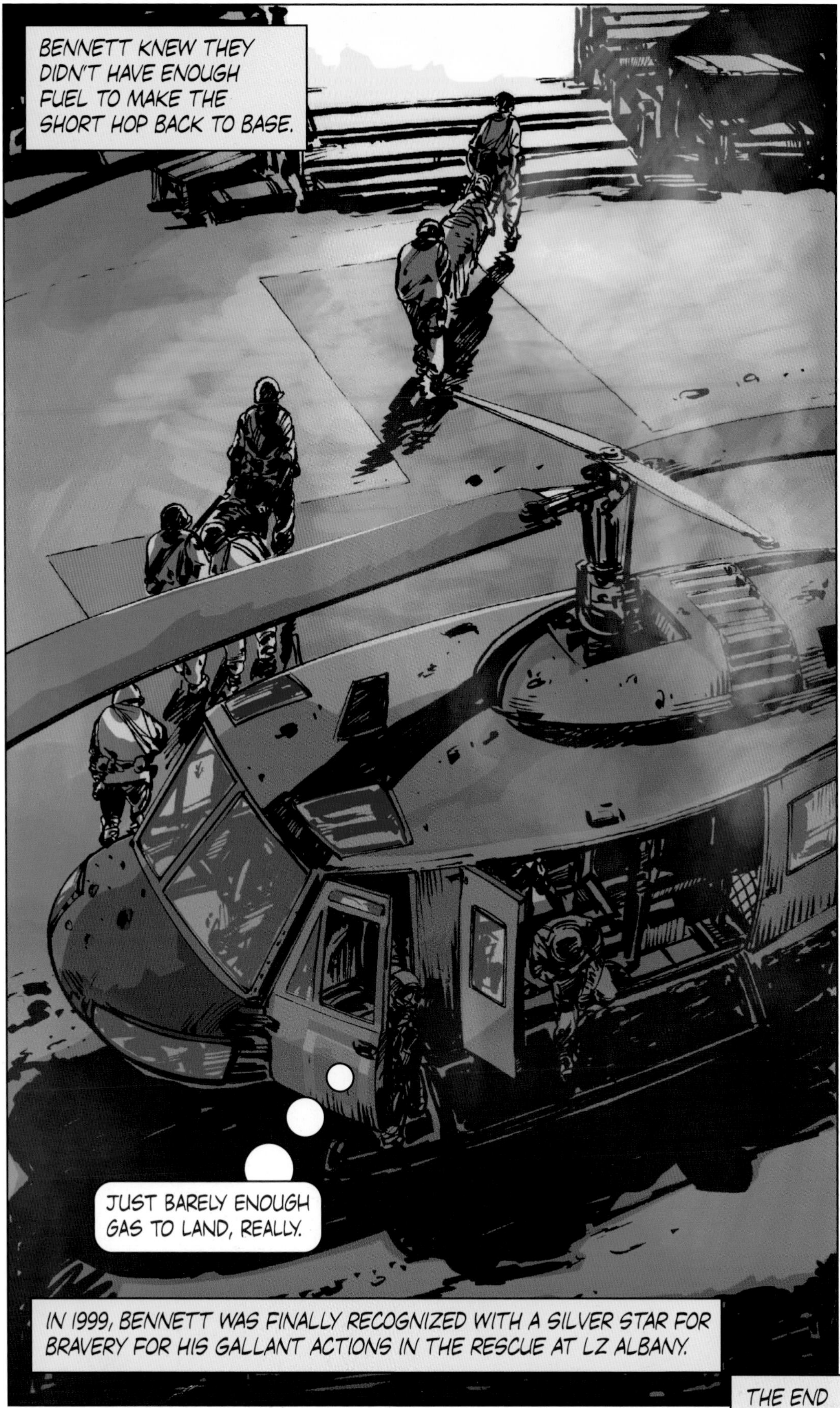
BENNETT KNEW THEY DIDN'T HAVE ENOUGH FUEL TO MAKE THE SHORT HOP BACK TO BASE.
JUST BARELY ENOUGH GAS TO LAND, REALLY.
IN 1999, BENNETT WAS FINALLY RECOGNIZED WITH A SILVER STAR FOR BRAVERY FOR HIS GALLANT ACTIONS IN THE RESCUE AT LZ ALBANY.

THE END

CLOSE CALL IN THE STREET WITHOUT JOY

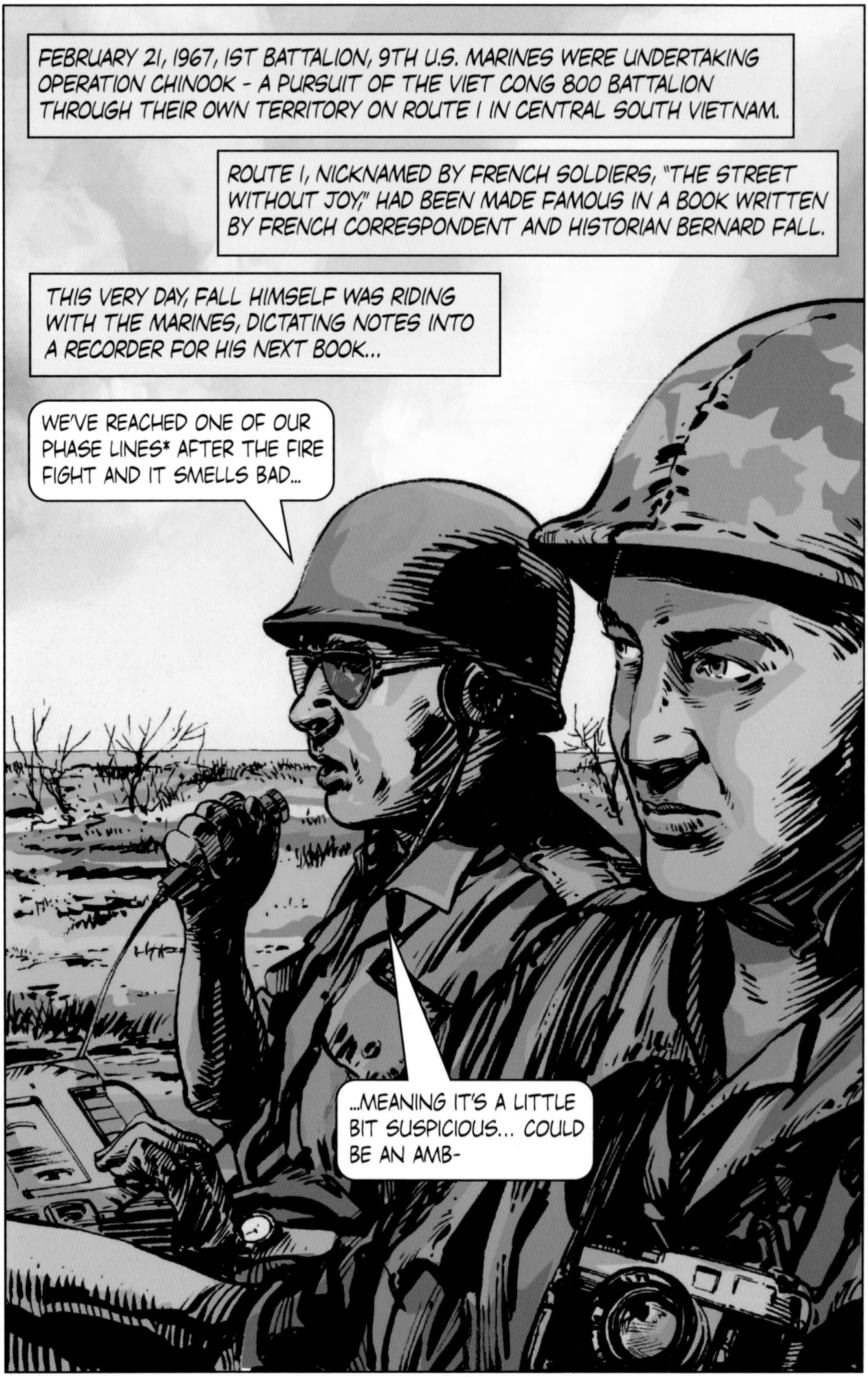
FEBRUARY 21, 1967, 1ST BATTALION, 9TH U.S. MARINES WERE UNDERTAKING OPERATION CHINOOK - A PURSUIT OF THE VIET CONG 800 BATTALION THROUGH THEIR OWN TERRITORY ON ROUTE 1 IN CENTRAL SOUTH VIETNAM.
ROUTE 1, NICKNAMED BY FRENCH SOLDIERS, "THE STREET WITHOUT JOY," HAD BEEN MADE FAMOUS IN A BOOK WRITTEN BY FRENCH CORRESPONDENT AND HISTORIAN BERNARD FALL.
THIS VERY DAY, FALL HIMSELF WAS RIDING WITH THE MARINES, DICTATING NOTES INTO A RECORDER FOR HIS NEXT BOOK...
WE'VE REACHED ONE OF OUR PHASE LINES* AFTER THE FIRE FIGHT AND IT SMELLS BAD...
...MEANING IT'S A LITTLE BIT SUSPICIOUS... COULD BE AN AMB-

*MILITARY TERM FOR AN IMAGINARY BORDER THAT SHOWS WHO CONTROLS TERRITORY

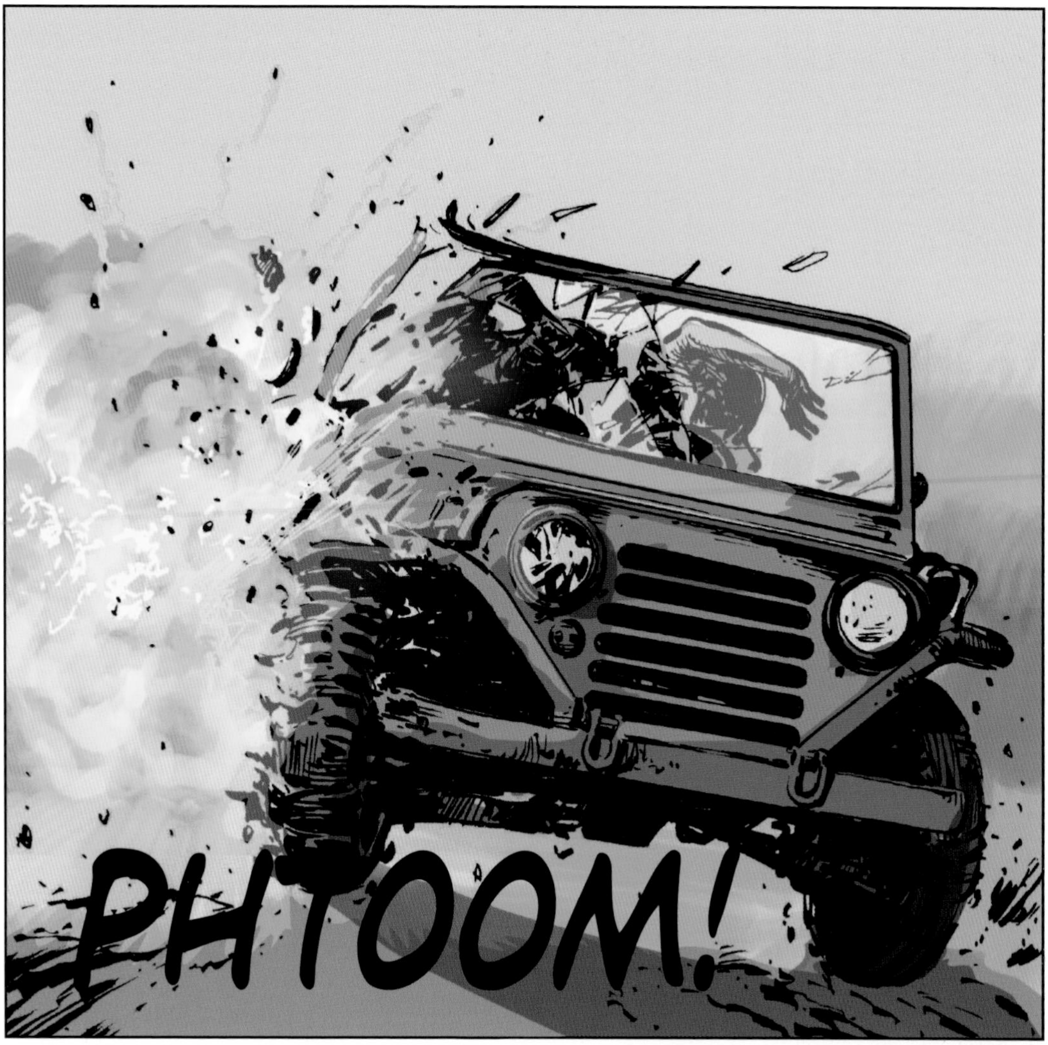
PHTOOM!

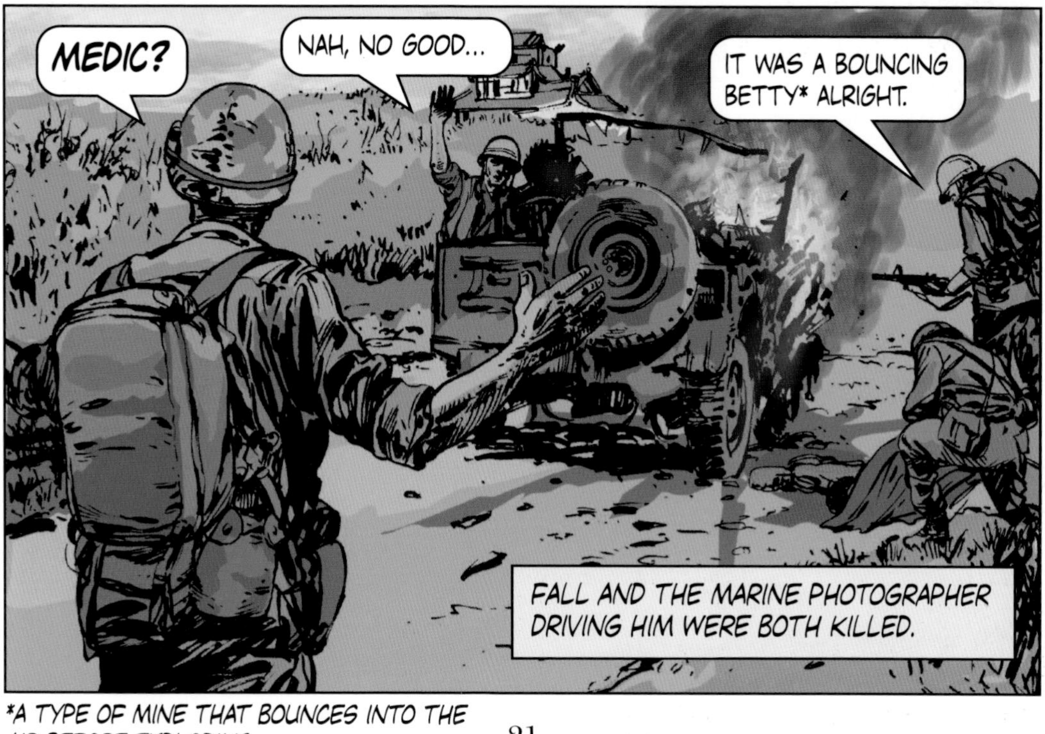
MEDIC?
NAH, NO GOOD...
IT WAS A BOUNCING BETTY* ALRIGHT.
FALL AND THE MARINE PHOTOGRAPHER DRIVING HIM WERE BOTH KILLED.

*A TYPE OF MINE THAT BOUNCES INTO THE AIR BEFORE EXPLODING.

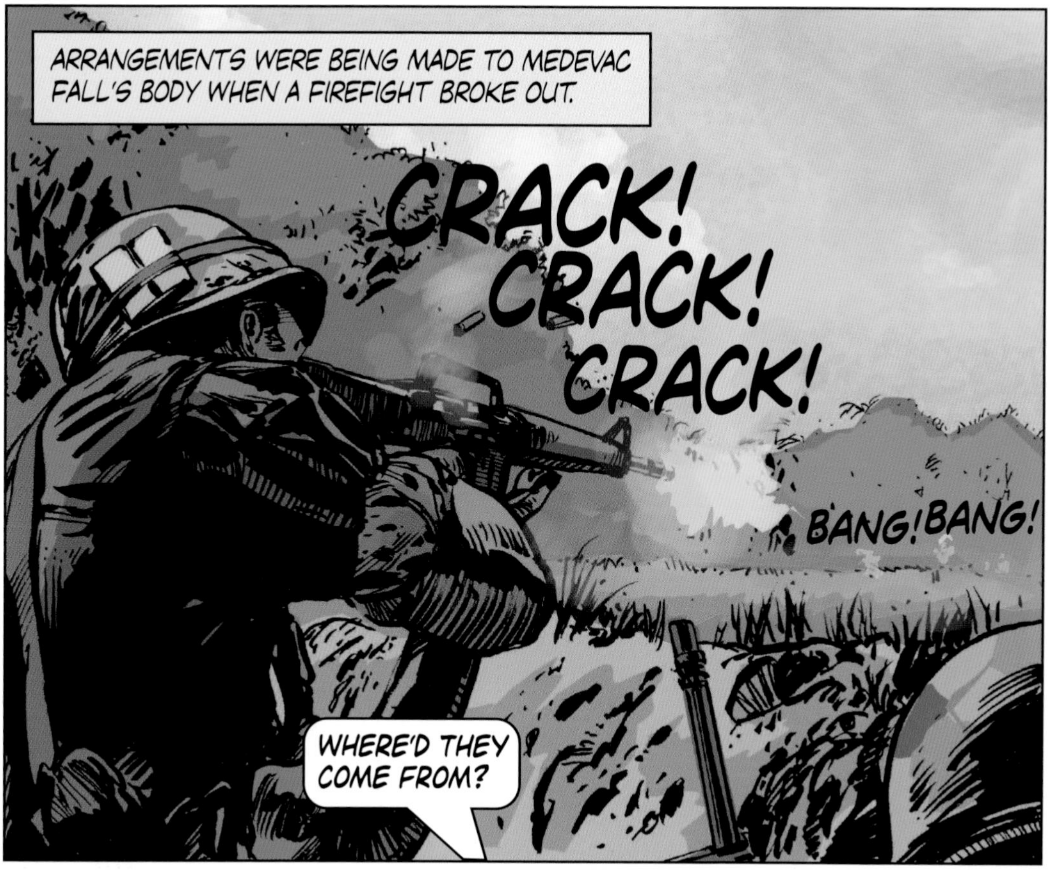
ARRANGEMENTS WERE BEING MADE TO MEDEVAC FALL'S BODY WHEN A FIREFIGHT BROKE OUT.
CRACK!
CRACK!
CRACK!
BANG! BANG!
WHERE'D THEY COME FROM?

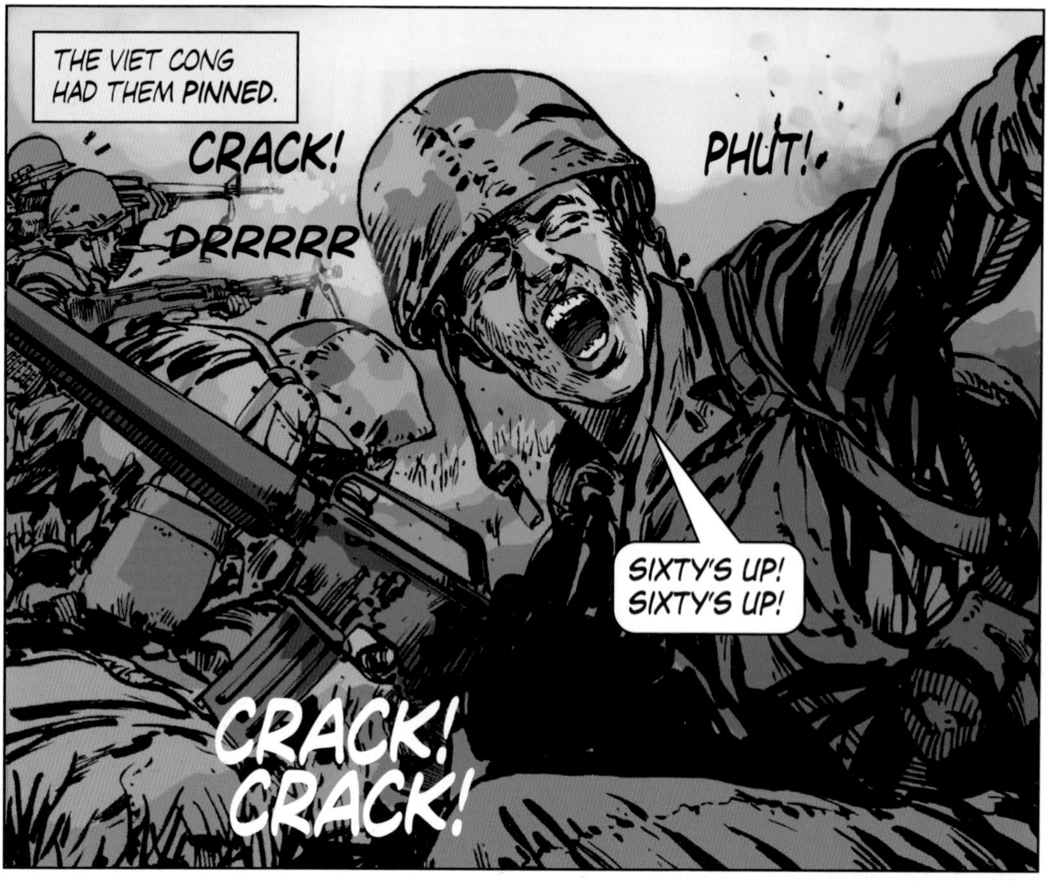
THE VIET CONG HAD THEM PINNED.
CRACK!
DRRRRR
PHUT!
SIXTY'S UP! SIXTY'S UP!
CRACK!
CRACK!

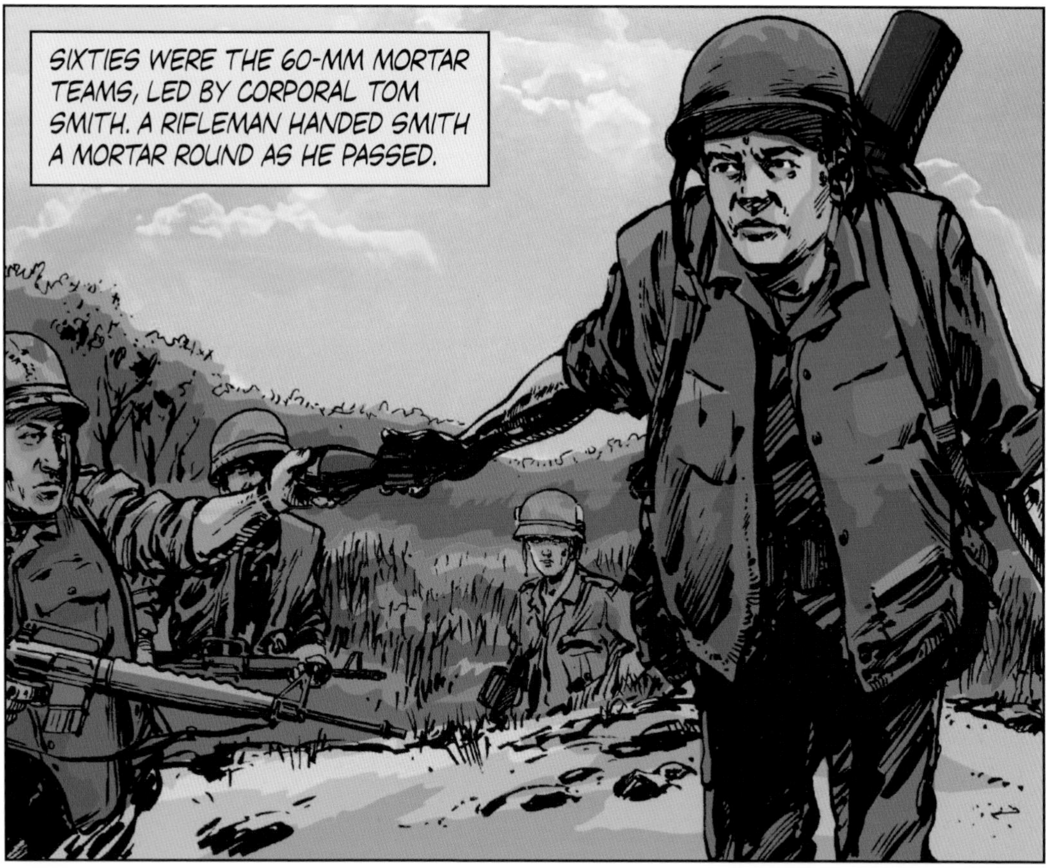
SIXTIES WERE THE 60-MM MORTAR TEAMS, LED BY CORPORAL TOM SMITH. A RIFLEMAN HANDED SMITH A MORTAR ROUND AS HE PASSED.

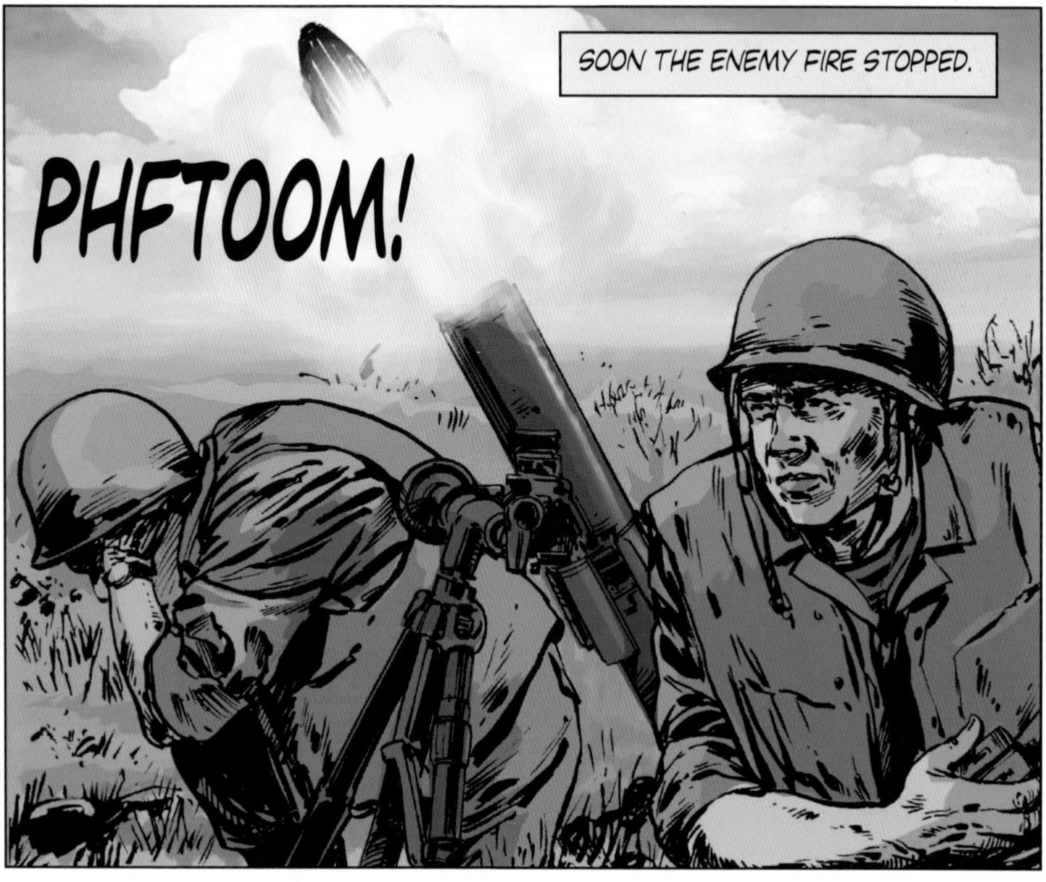
SOON THE ENEMY FIRE STOPPED.
PHFTOOM!

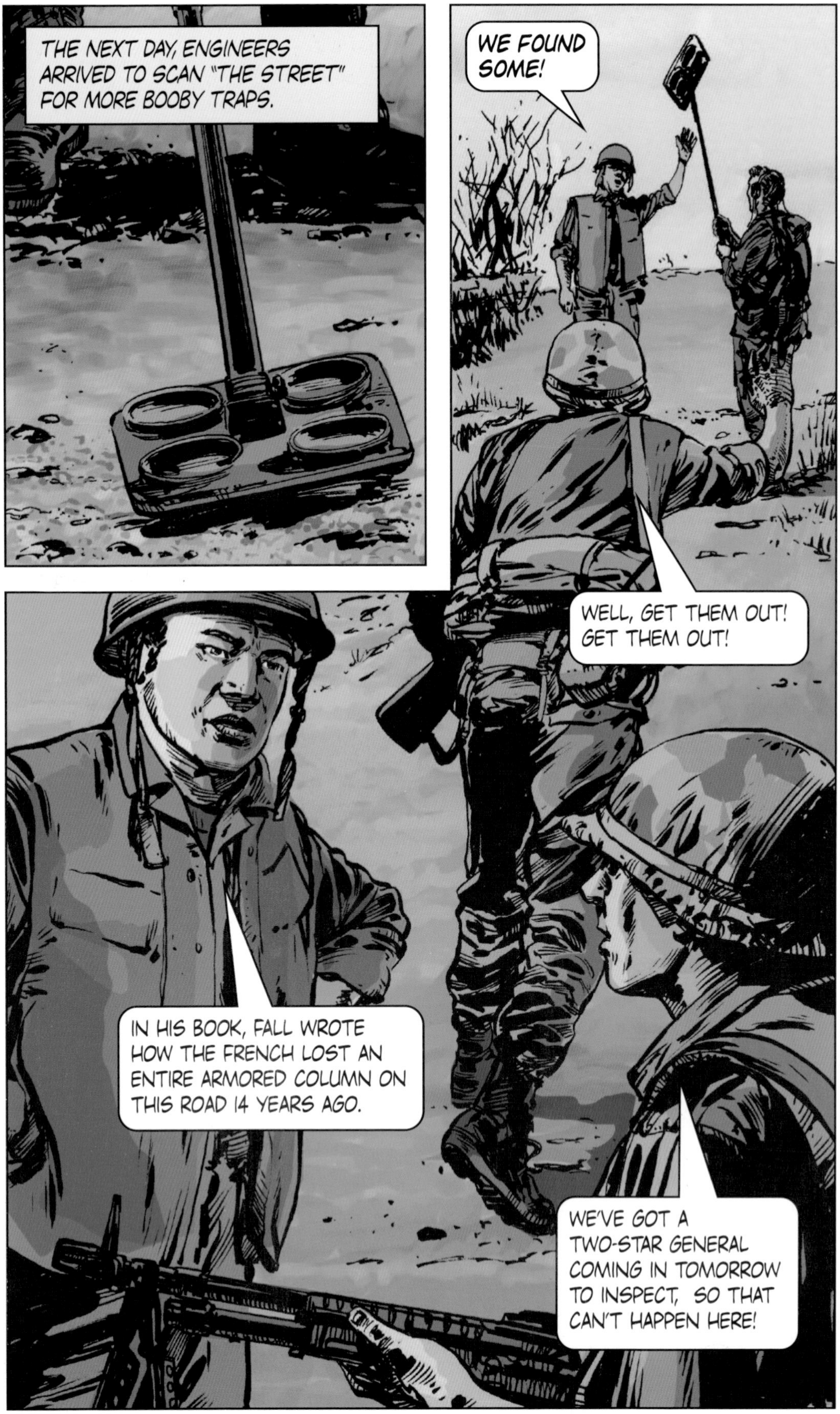
THE NEXT DAY, ENGINEERS ARRIVED TO SCAN "THE STREET" FOR MORE BOOBY TRAPS.
WE FOUND SOME!
WELL, GET THEM OUT! GET THEM OUT!
IN HIS BOOK, FALL WROTE HOW THE FRENCH LOST AN ENTIRE ARMORED COLUMN ON THIS ROAD 14 YEARS AGO.
WE'VE GOT A TWO-STAR GENERAL COMING IN TOMORROW TO INSPECT, SO THAT CAN'T HAPPEN HERE!

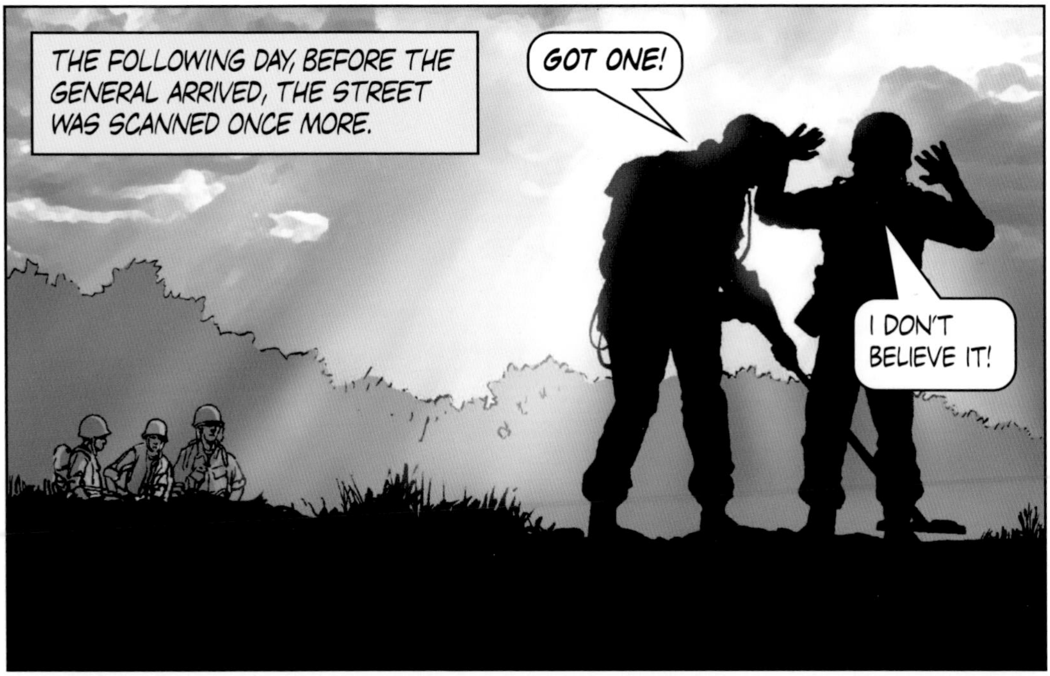
THE FOLLOWING DAY, BEFORE THE GENERAL ARRIVED, THE STREET WAS SCANNED ONCE MORE.
GOT ONE!
I DON'T BELIEVE IT!

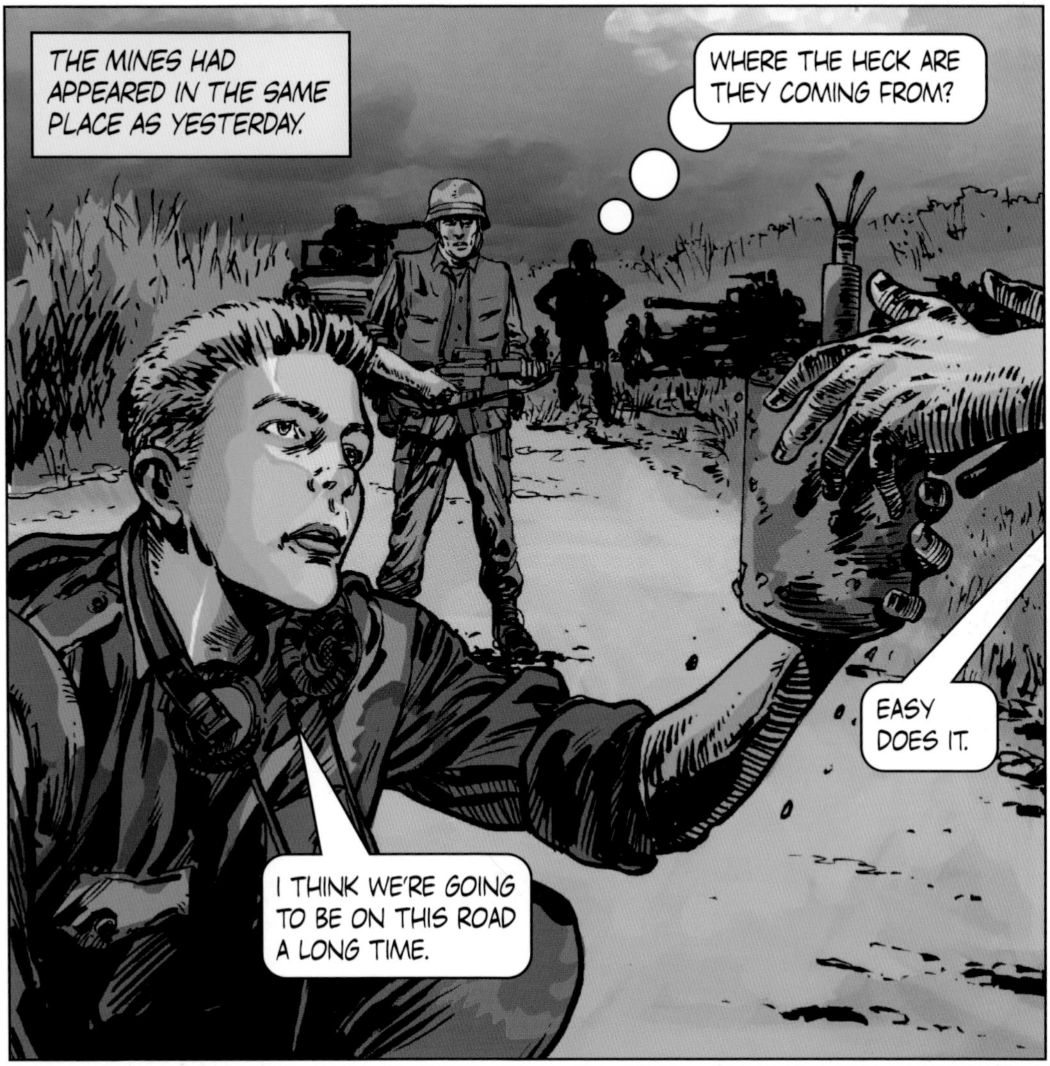
THE MINES HAD APPEARED IN THE SAME PLACE AS YESTERDAY.
WHERE THE HECK ARE THEY COMING FROM?
EASY DOES IT.
I THINK WE'RE GOING TO BE ON THIS ROAD A LONG TIME.

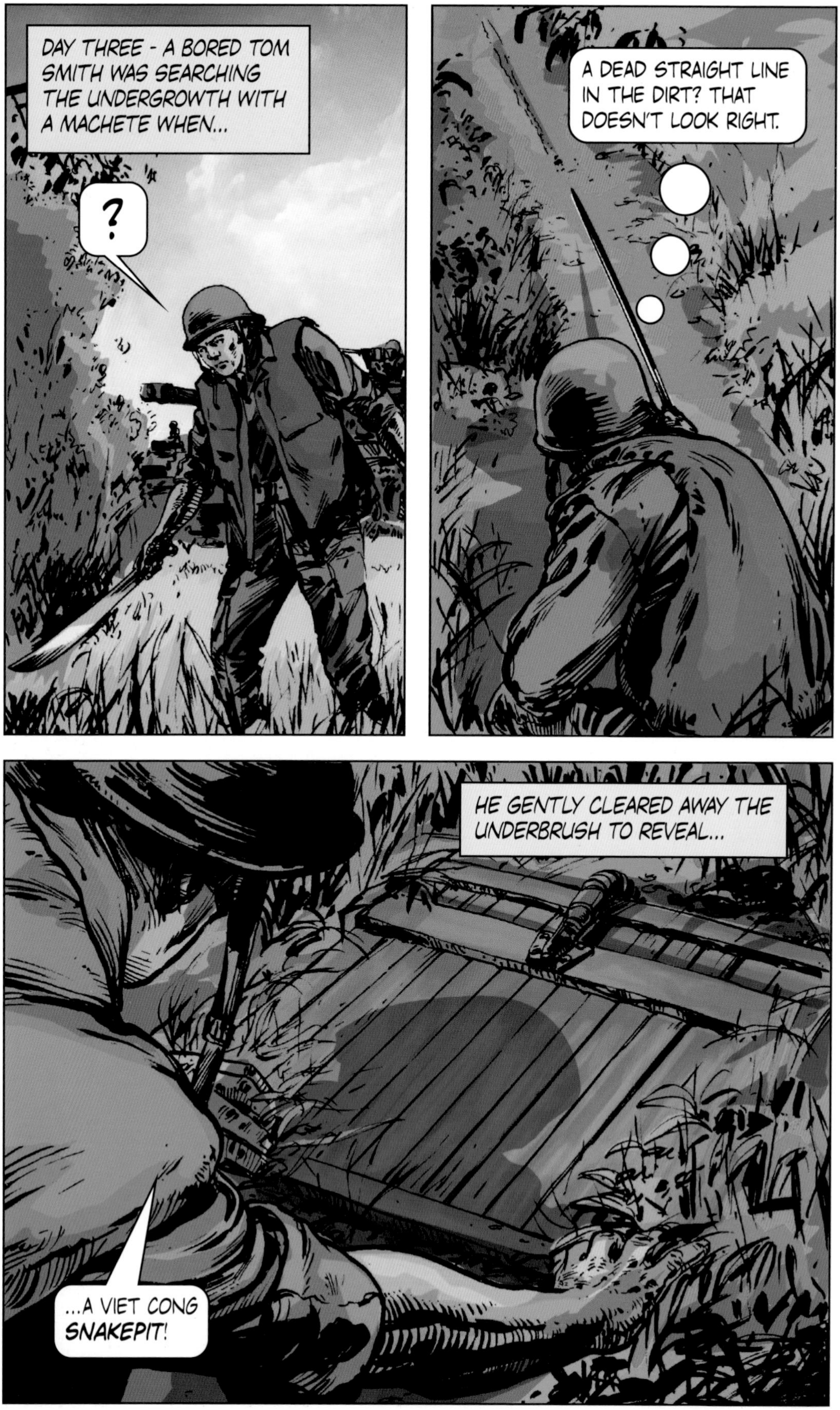
DAY THREE - A BORED TOM SMITH WAS SEARCHING THE UNDERGROWTH WITH A MACHETE WHEN...
?
A DEAD STRAIGHT LINE IN THE DIRT? THAT DOESN'T LOOK RIGHT.
HE GENTLY CLEARED AWAY THE UNDERBRUSH TO REVEAL...
...A VIET CONG **SNAKEPIT**!

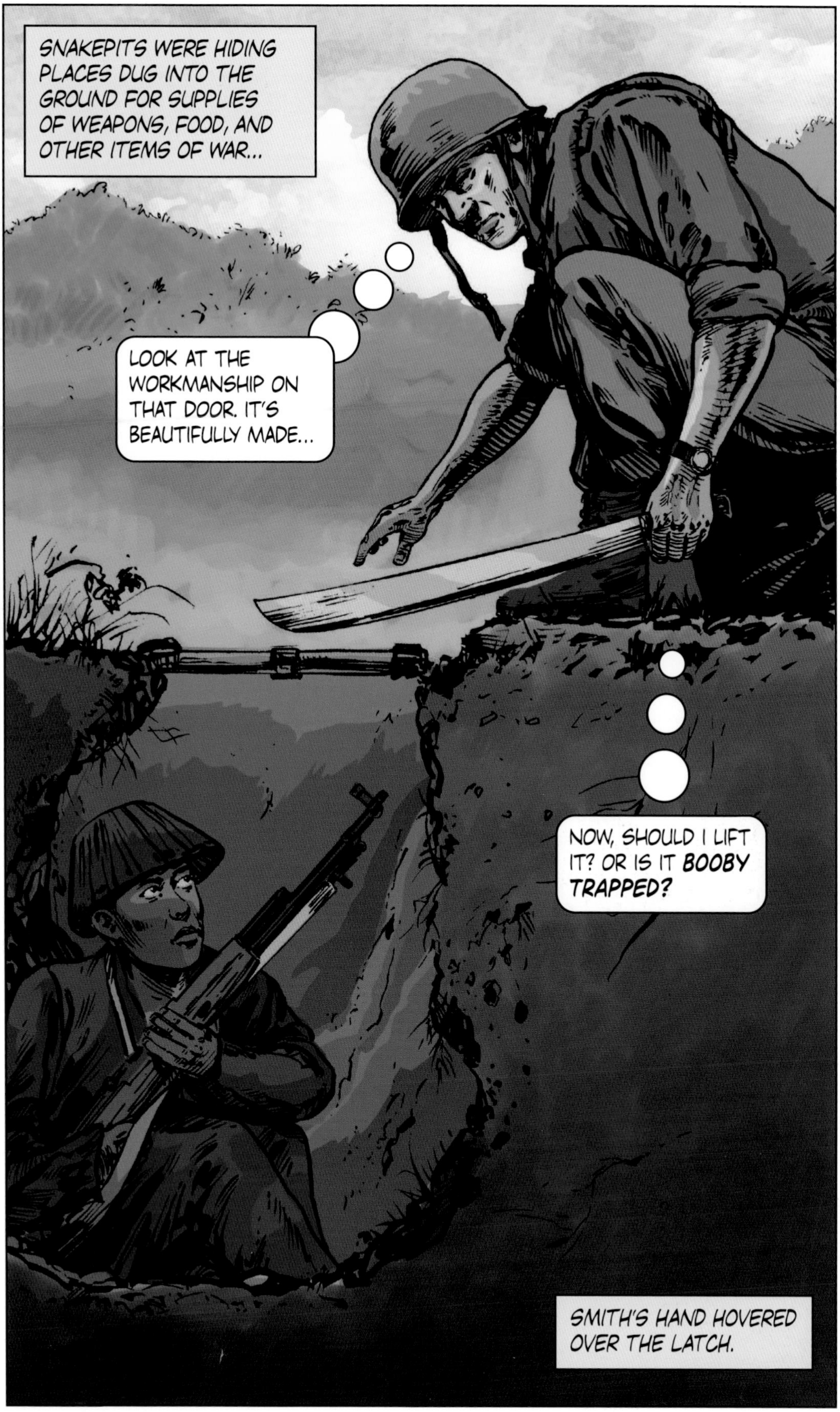
SNAKEPITS WERE HIDING PLACES DUG INTO THE GROUND FOR SUPPLIES OF WEAPONS, FOOD, AND OTHER ITEMS OF WAR...
LOOK AT THE WORKMANSHIP ON THAT DOOR. IT'S BEAUTIFULLY MADE...
NOW, SHOULD I LIFT IT? OR IS IT BOOBY TRAPPED?
SMITH'S HAND HOVERED OVER THE LATCH.

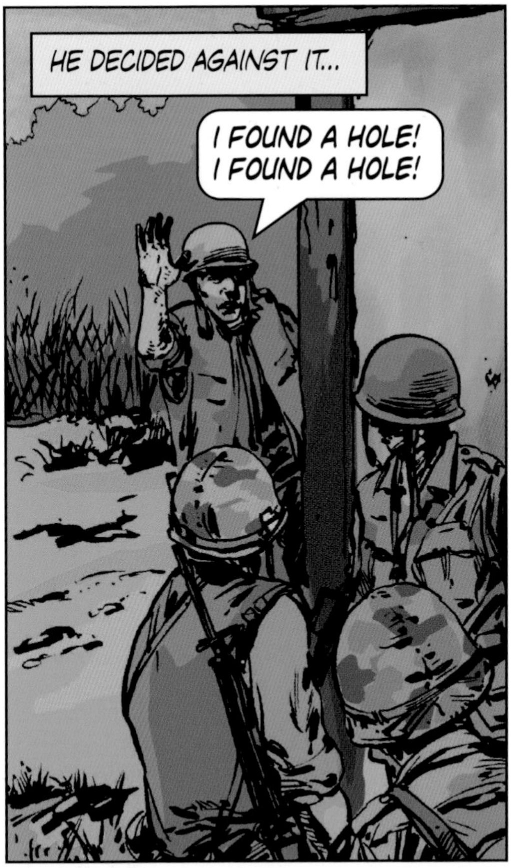
HE DECIDED AGAINST IT...
I FOUND A HOLE! I FOUND A HOLE!

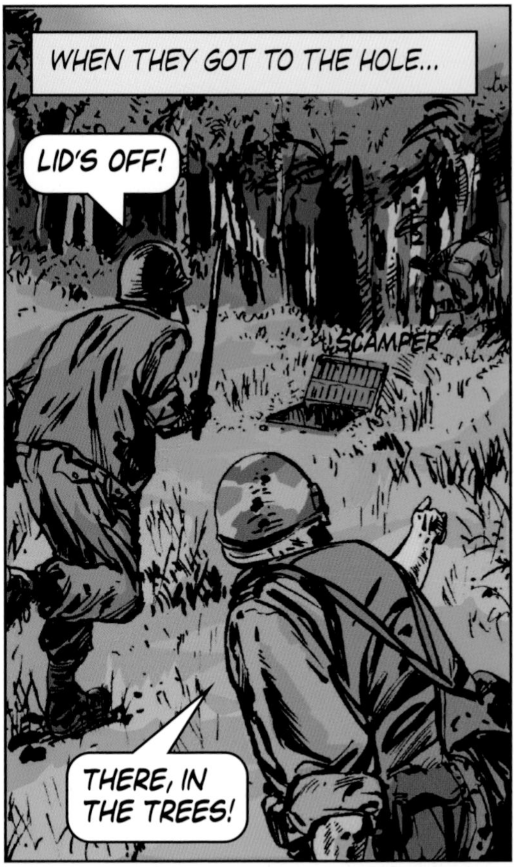
WHEN THEY GOT TO THE HOLE...
LID'S OFF!
SCAMPER
THERE, IN THE TREES!

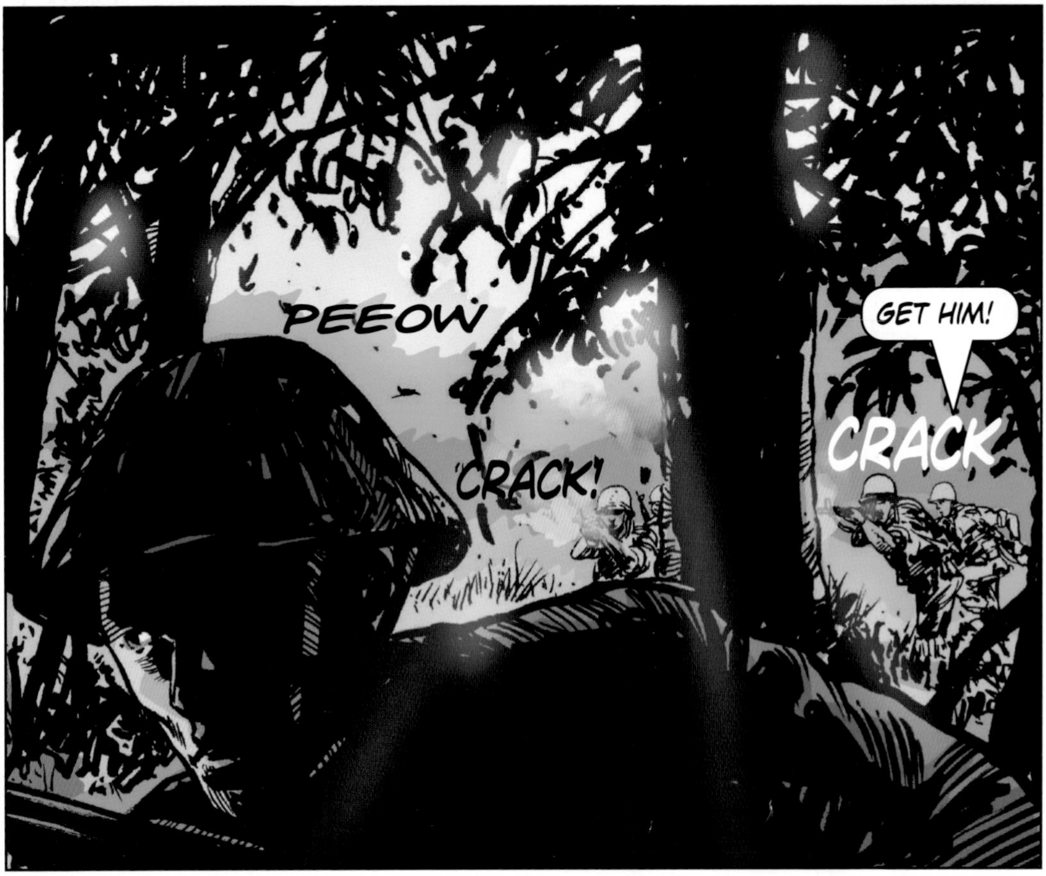
PEEOW
CRACK!
GET HIM!
CRACK

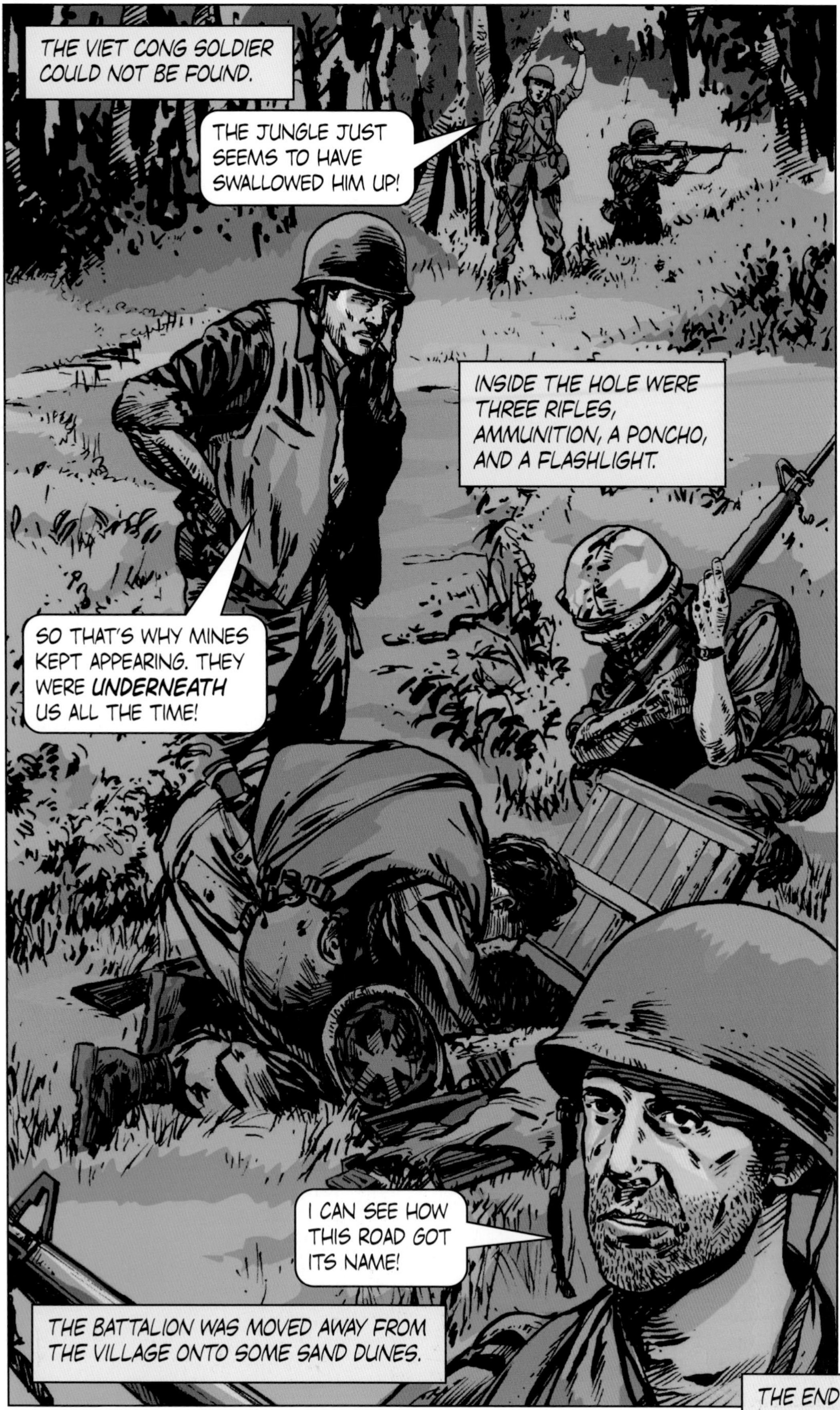
THE VIET CONG SOLDIER COULD NOT BE FOUND.
THE JUNGLE JUST SEEMS TO HAVE SWALLOWED HIM UP!
INSIDE THE HOLE WERE THREE RIFLES, AMMUNITION, A PONCHO, AND A FLASHLIGHT.
SO THAT'S WHY MINES KEPT APPEARING. THEY WERE **UNDERNEATH** US ALL THE TIME!
I CAN SEE HOW THIS ROAD GOT ITS NAME!
THE BATTALION WAS MOVED AWAY FROM THE VILLAGE ONTO SOME SAND DUNES.

THE END

DOUBLE GUN KILL

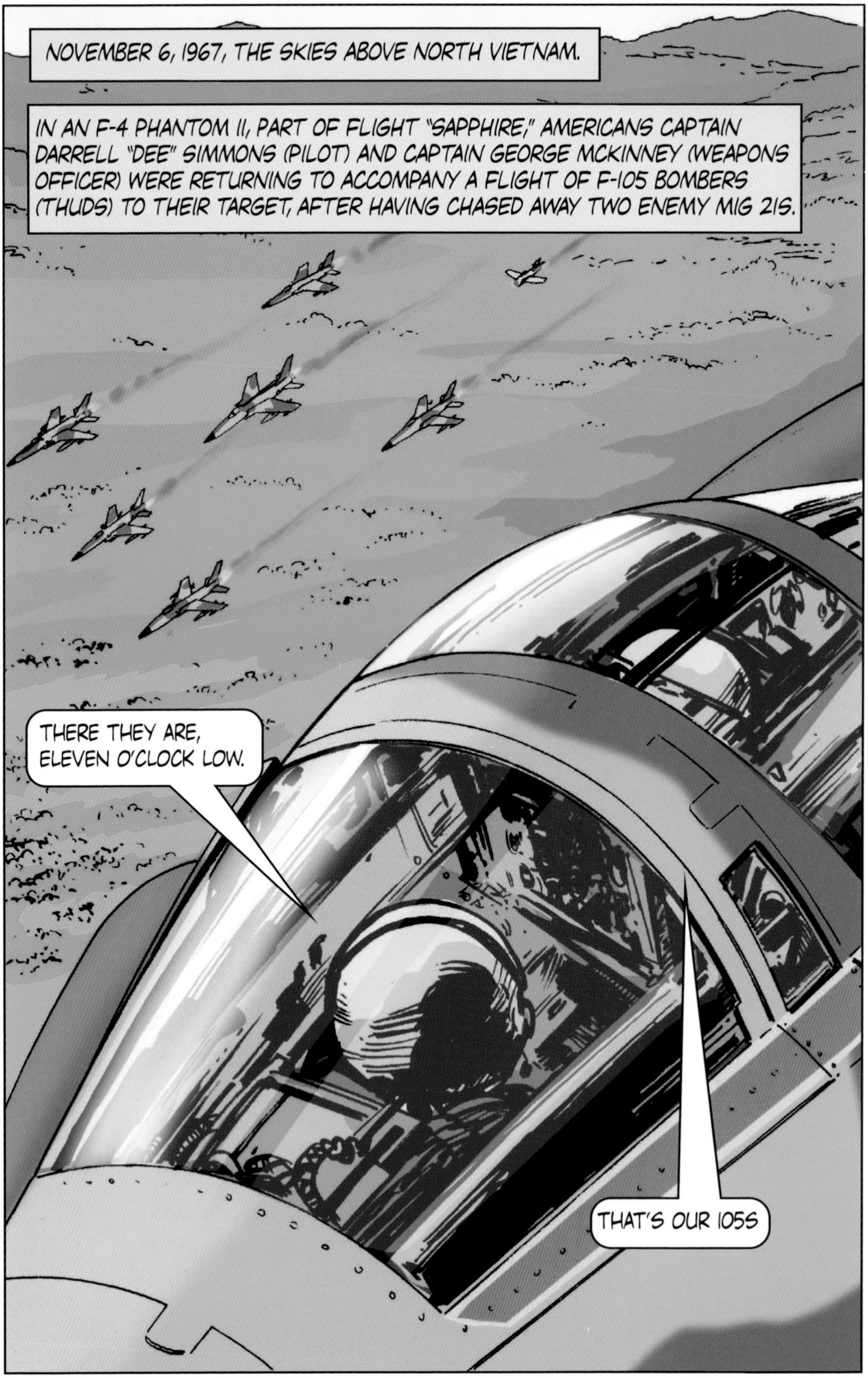

NOVEMBER 6, 1967, THE SKIES ABOVE NORTH VIETNAM.
IN AN F-4 PHANTOM II, PART OF FLIGHT "SAPPHIRE," AMERICANS CAPTAIN DARRELL "DEE" SIMMONS (PILOT) AND CAPTAIN GEORGE MCKINNEY (WEAPONS OFFICER) WERE RETURNING TO ACCOMPANY A FLIGHT OF F-105 BOMBERS (THUDS) TO THEIR TARGET, AFTER HAVING CHASED AWAY TWO ENEMY MIG 21S.
THERE THEY ARE, ELEVEN O'CLOCK LOW.
THAT'S OUR 105S

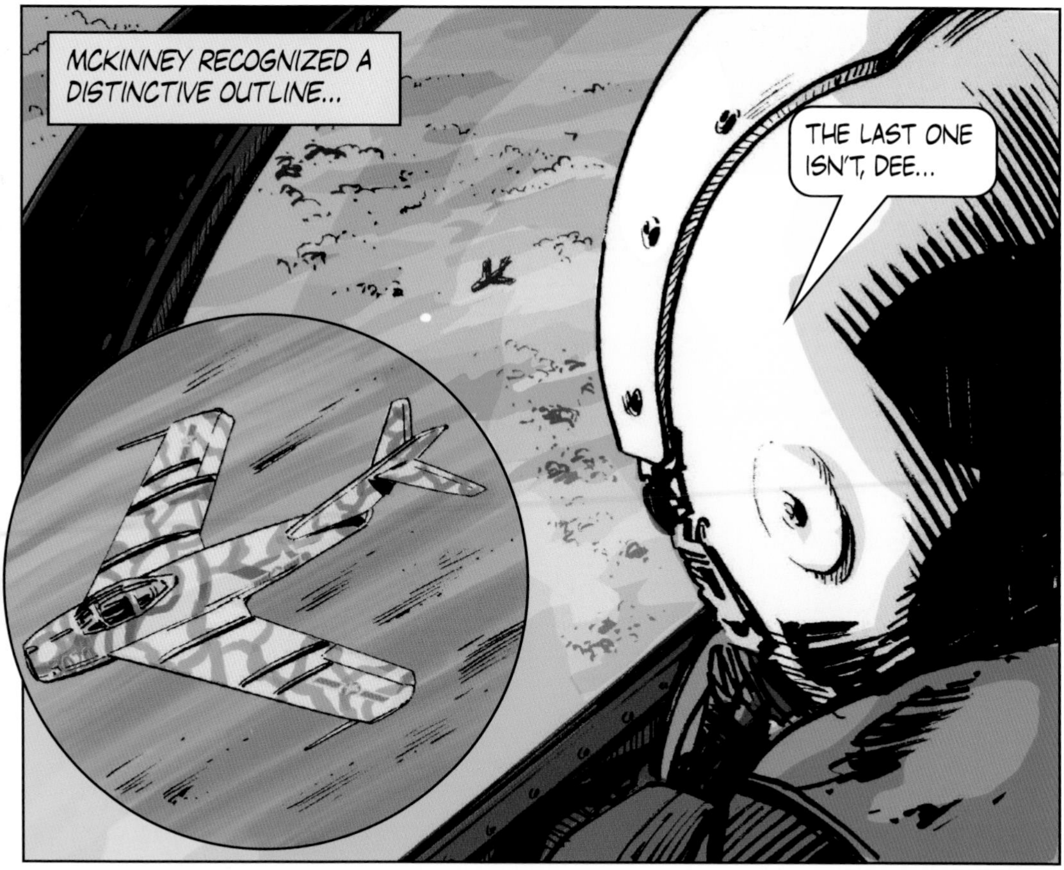
MCKINNEY RECOGNIZED A DISTINCTIVE OUTLINE...
THE LAST ONE ISN'T, DEE...

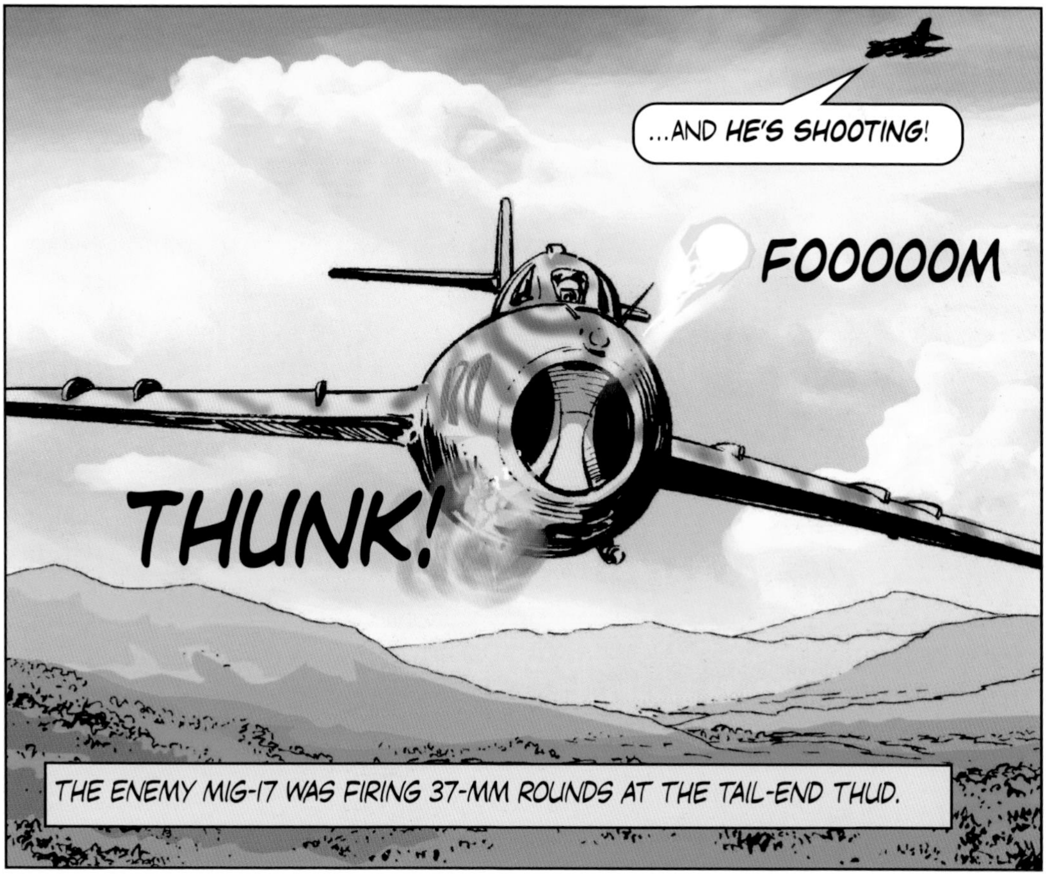
...AND HE'S SHOOTING!
FOOOOOM
THUNK!
THE ENEMY MIG-17 WAS FIRING 37-MM ROUNDS AT THE TAIL-END THUD.

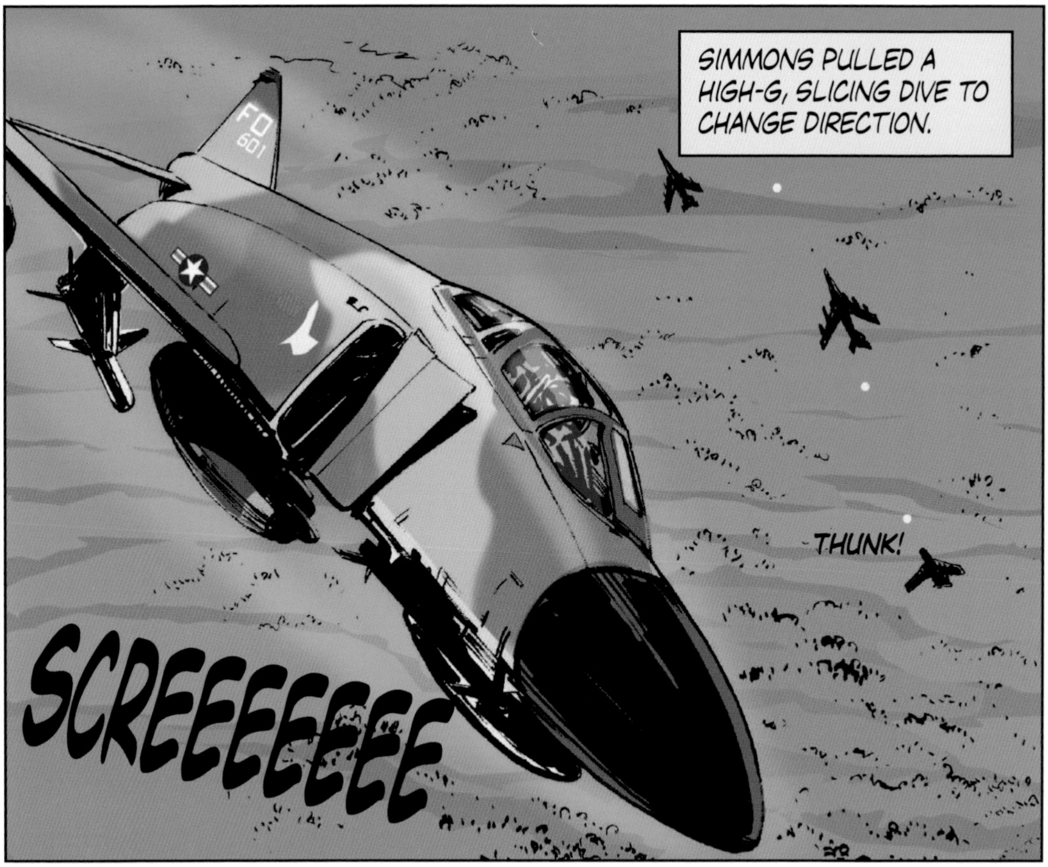
SIMMONS PULLED A HIGH-G, SLICING DIVE TO CHANGE DIRECTION.
THUNK!
SCREEEEEEEE
FO 601

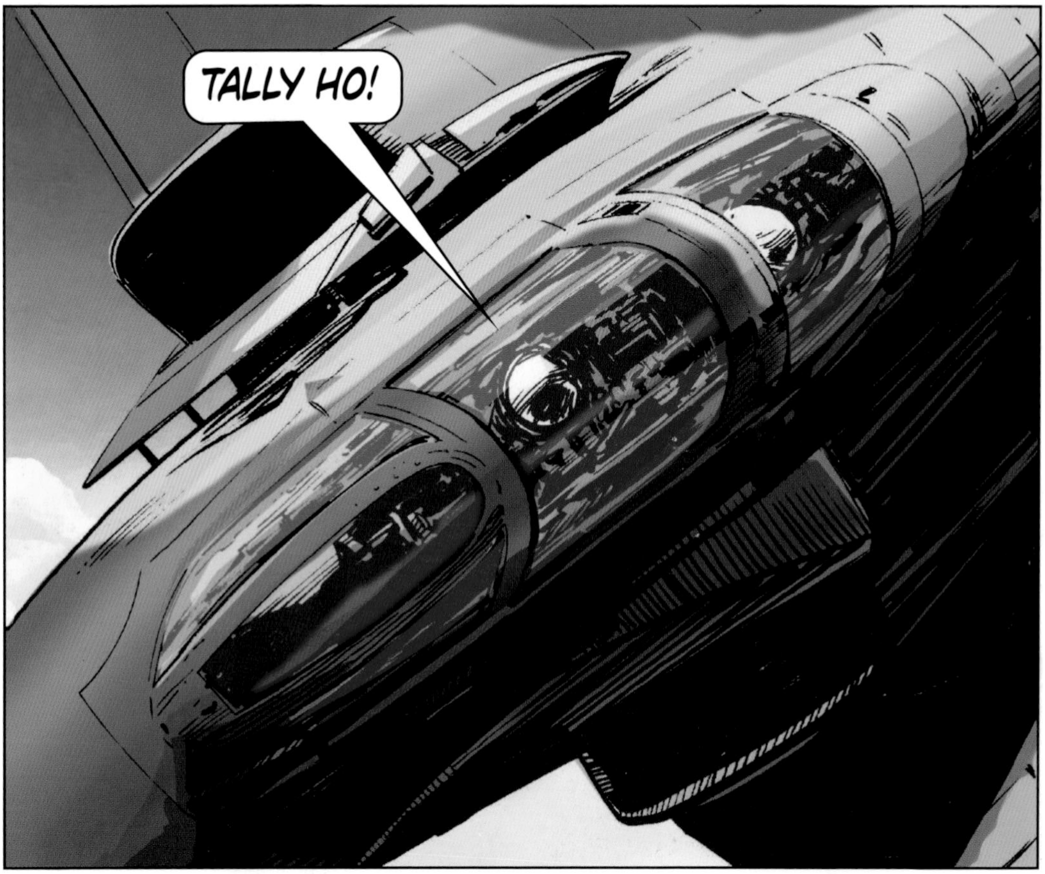
TALLY HO!

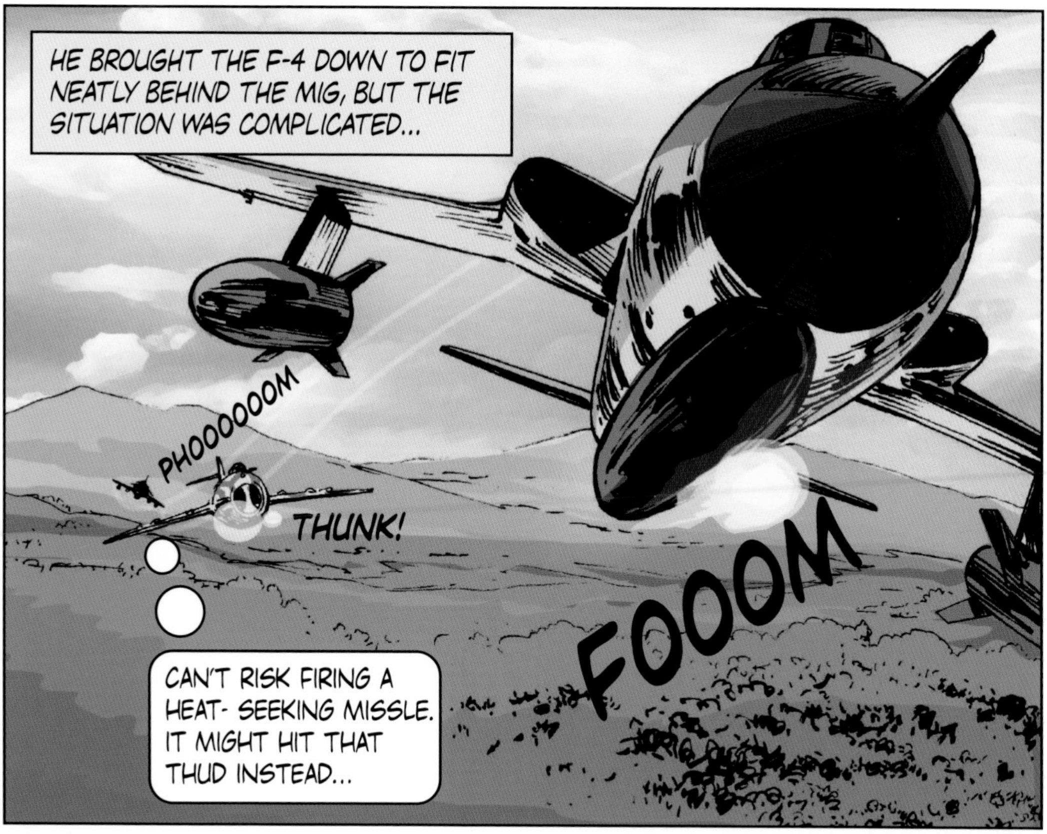
HE BROUGHT THE F-4 DOWN TO FIT NEATLY BEHIND THE MIG, BUT THE SITUATION WAS COMPLICATED...
PHOOOOOOM
THUNK!
FOOOM
CAN'T RISK FIRING A HEAT- SEEKING MISSLE. IT MIGHT HIT THAT THUD INSTEAD...

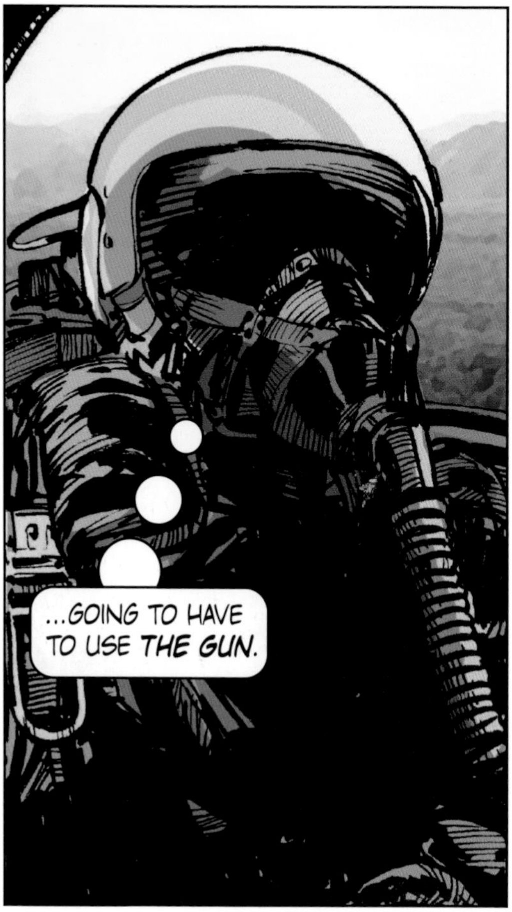
...GOING TO HAVE TO USE THE GUN.

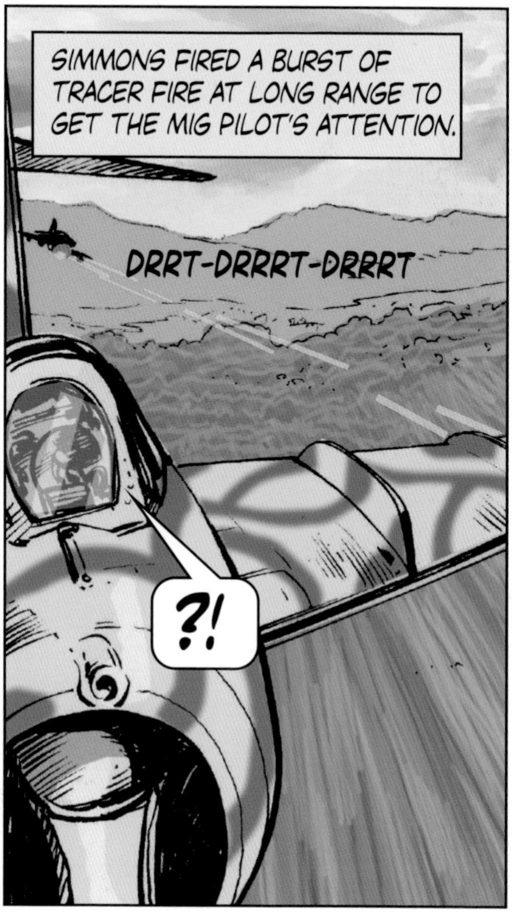
SIMMONS FIRED A BURST OF TRACER FIRE AT LONG RANGE TO GET THE MIG PILOT'S ATTENTION.
DRRT-DRRRT-DRRRT
?!

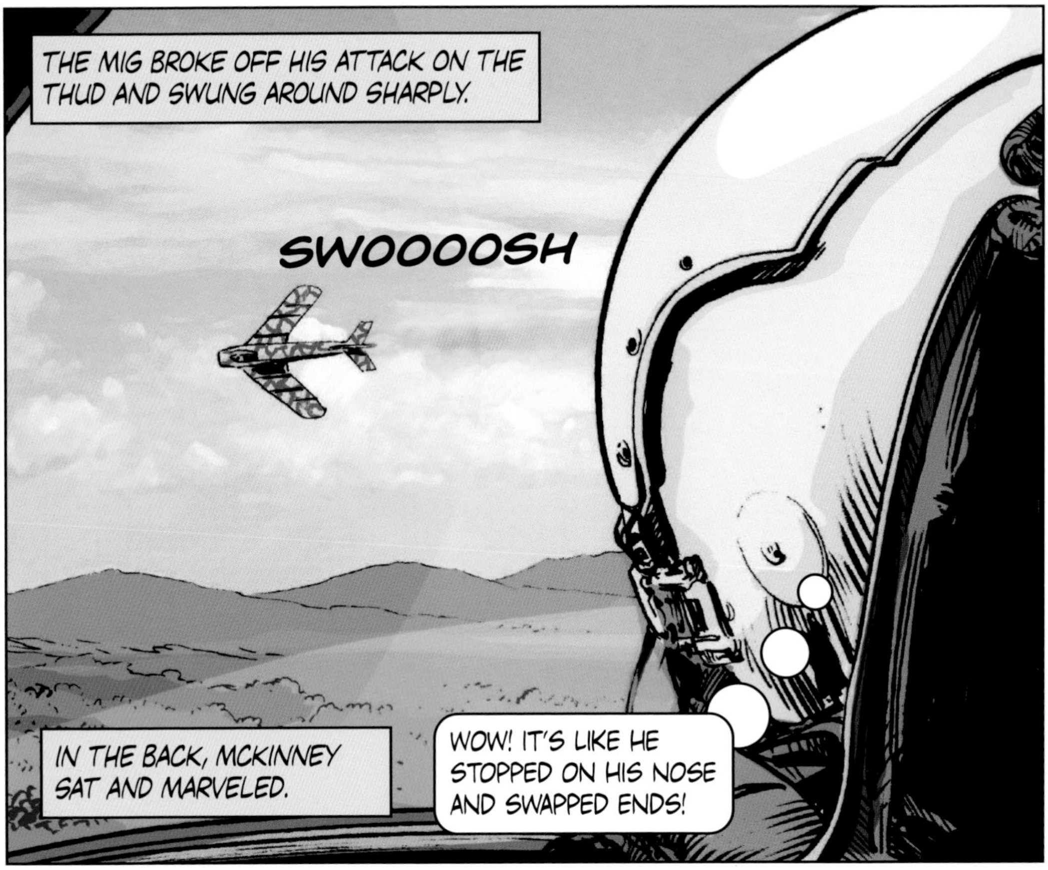
THE MIG BROKE OFF HIS ATTACK ON THE THUD AND SWUNG AROUND SHARPLY.
SWOOOOSH
IN THE BACK, MCKINNEY SAT AND MARVELED.
WOW! IT'S LIKE HE STOPPED ON HIS NOSE AND SWAPPED ENDS!

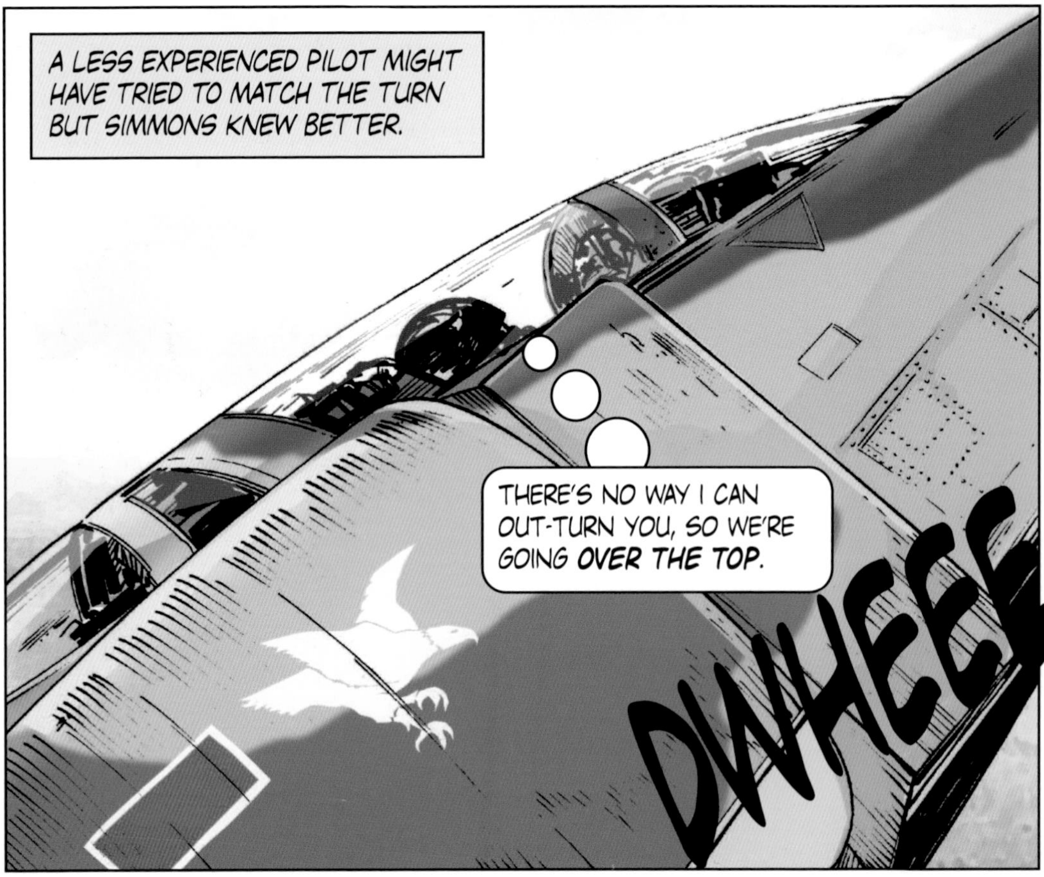
A LESS EXPERIENCED PILOT MIGHT HAVE TRIED TO MATCH THE TURN BUT SIMMONS KNEW BETTER.
THERE'S NO WAY I CAN OUT-TURN YOU, SO WE'RE GOING **OVER THE TOP**.
DWHEEE

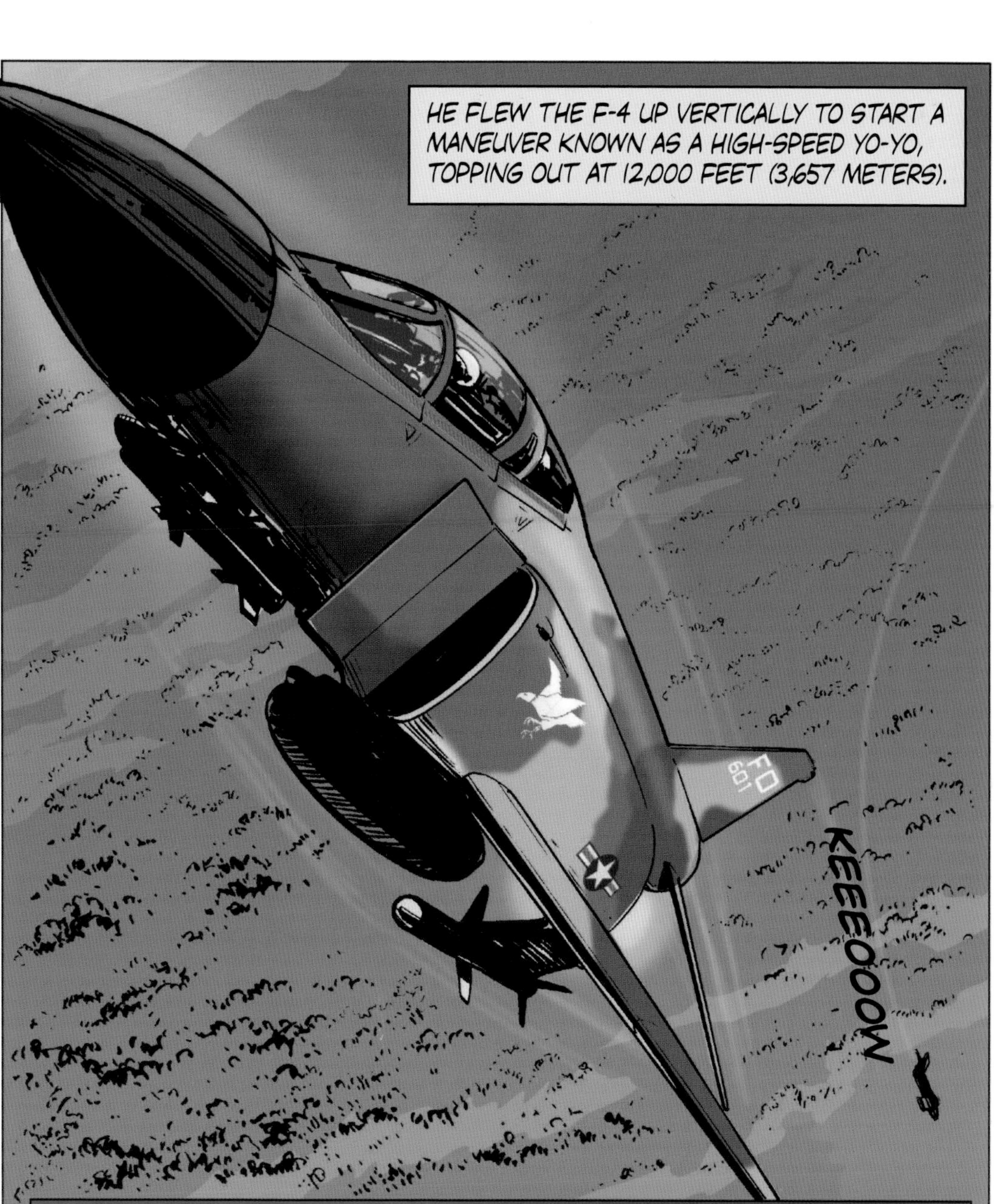
HE FLEW THE F-4 UP VERTICALLY TO START A MANEUVER KNOWN AS A HIGH-SPEED YO-YO, TOPPING OUT AT 12,000 FEET (3,657 METERS).
FD 601
KEEEOOOW

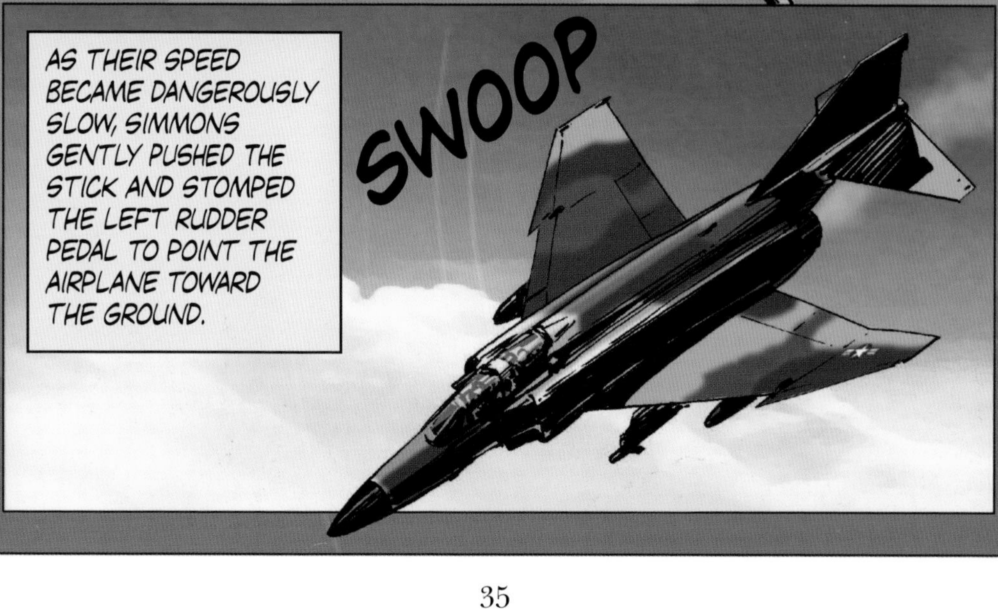
AS THEIR SPEED BECAME DANGEROUSLY SLOW, SIMMONS GENTLY PUSHED THE STICK AND STOMPED THE LEFT RUDDER PEDAL TO POINT THE AIRPLANE TOWARD THE GROUND.
SWOOP

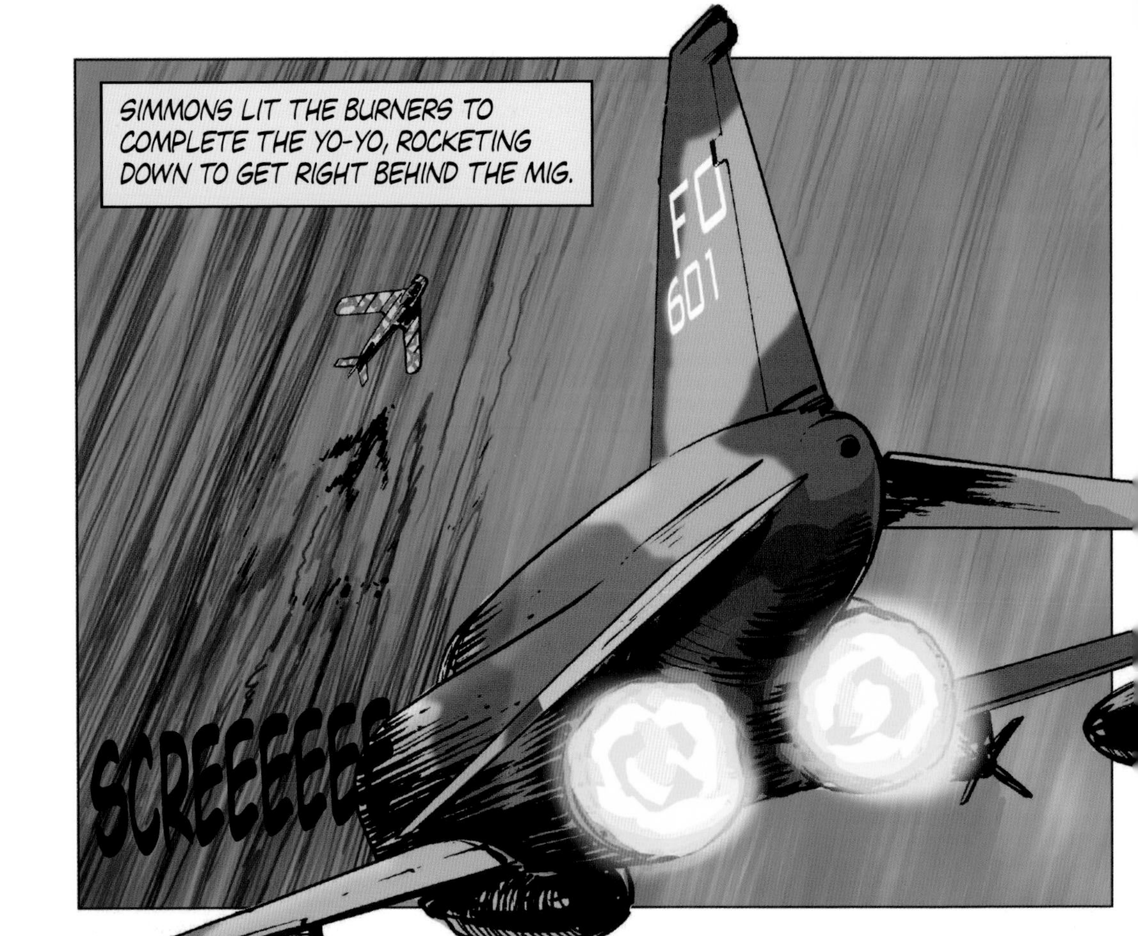
SIMMONS LIT THE BURNERS TO COMPLETE THE YO-YO, ROCKETING DOWN TO GET RIGHT BEHIND THE MIG.
FO
601
SCREEEEEE

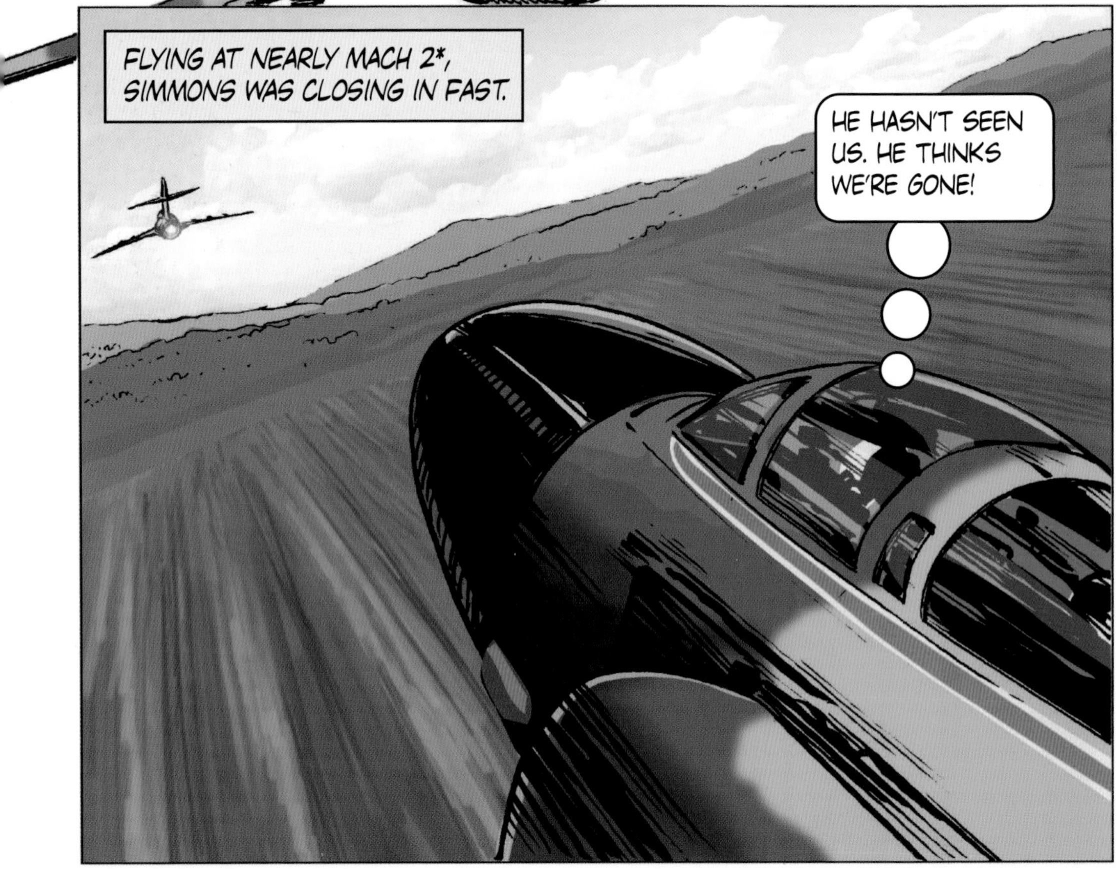
FLYING AT NEARLY MACH 2*, SIMMONS WAS CLOSING IN FAST.
HE HASN'T SEEN US. HE THINKS WE'RE GONE!

*1,536 MILES PER HOUR (2,471 KILOMETERS PER HOUR)

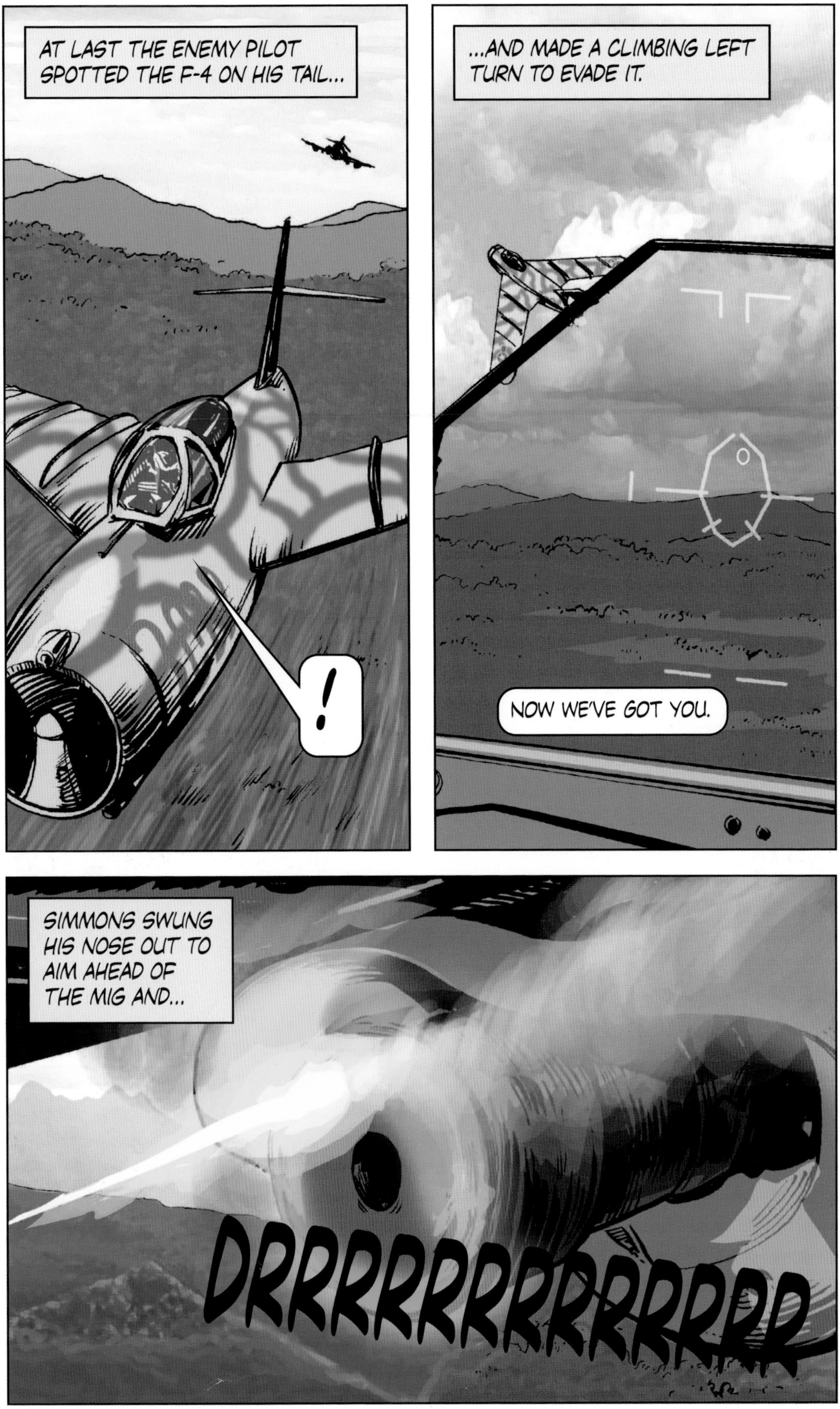
AT LAST THE ENEMY PILOT SPOTTED THE F-4 ON HIS TAIL...
!
...AND MADE A CLIMBING LEFT TURN TO EVADE IT.
NOW WE'VE GOT YOU.
SIMMONS SWUNG HIS NOSE OUT TO AIM AHEAD OF THE MIG AND...
DRRRRRRRRRRRRRR

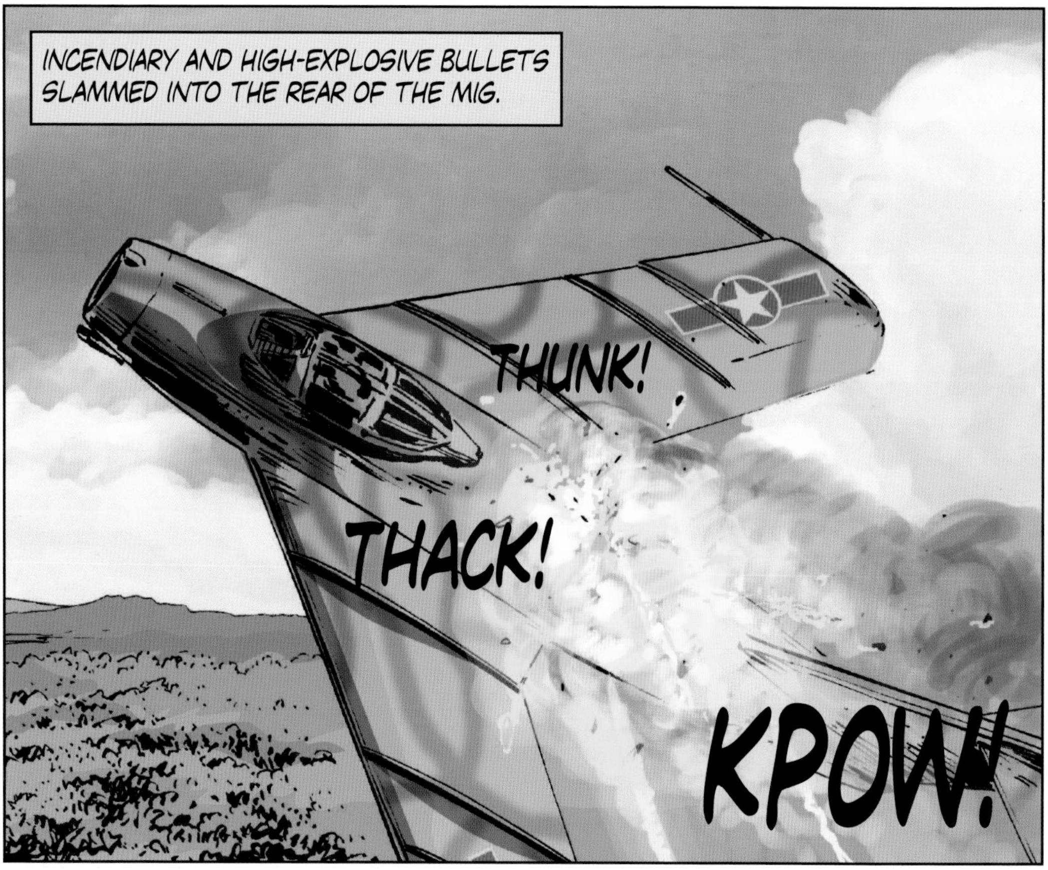
INCENDIARY AND HIGH-EXPLOSIVE BULLETS SLAMMED INTO THE REAR OF THE MIG.
THUNK!
THACK!
KPOW!

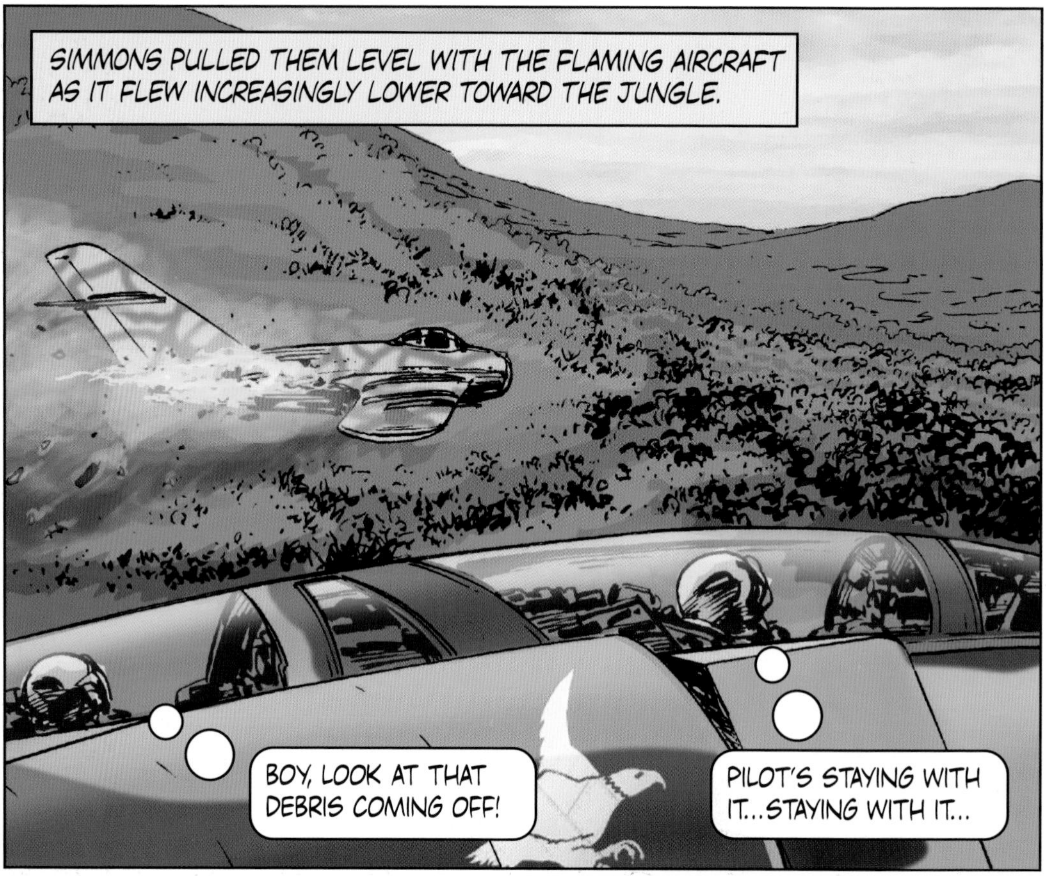
SIMMONS PULLED THEM LEVEL WITH THE FLAMING AIRCRAFT AS IT FLEW INCREASINGLY LOWER TOWARD THE JUNGLE.
BOY, LOOK AT THAT DEBRIS COMING OFF!
PILOT'S STAYING WITH IT...STAYING WITH IT...

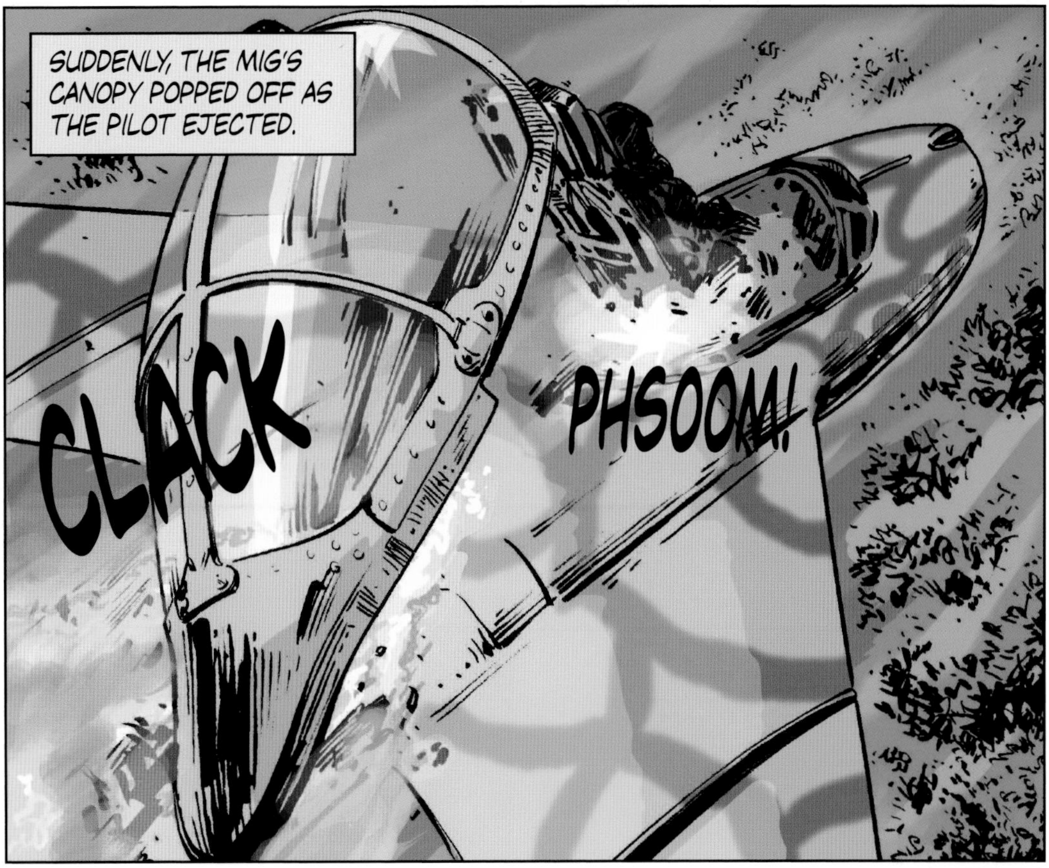
SUDDENLY, THE MIG'S CANOPY POPPED OFF AS THE PILOT EJECTED.
CLACK
PHSOOM!

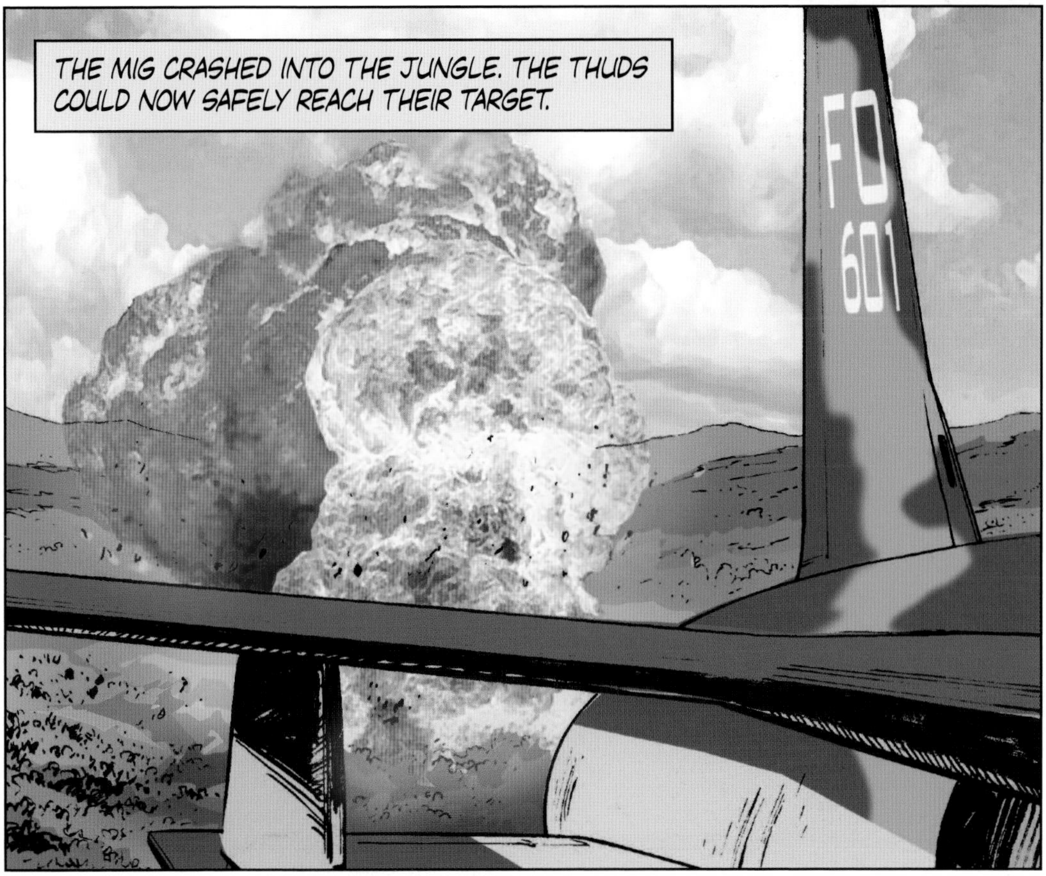
THE MIG CRASHED INTO THE JUNGLE. THE THUDS COULD NOW SAFELY REACH THEIR TARGET.
FO
601

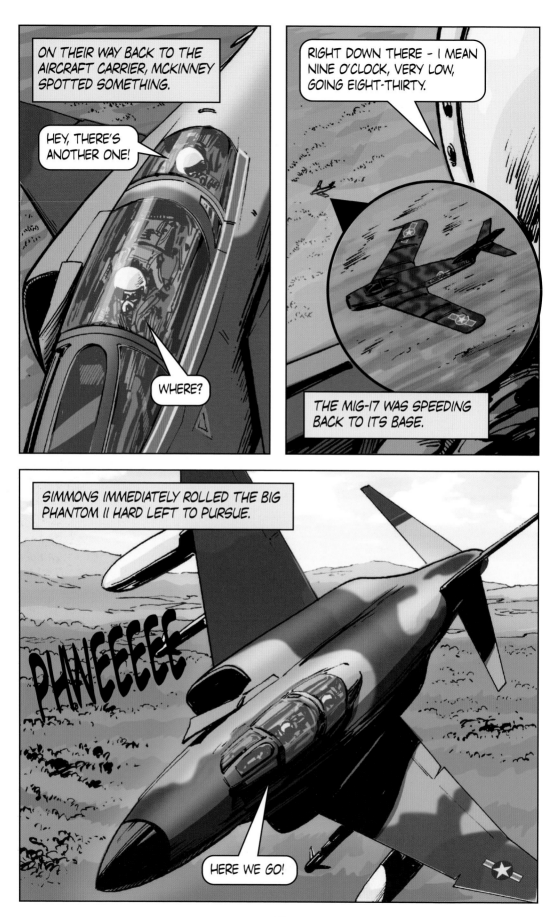

ON THEIR WAY BACK TO THE AIRCRAFT CARRIER, MCKINNEY SPOTTED SOMETHING.

HEY, THERE'S ANOTHER ONE!

WHERE?

RIGHT DOWN THERE – I MEAN NINE O'CLOCK, VERY LOW, GOING EIGHT-THIRTY.

THE MIG-17 WAS SPEEDING BACK TO ITS BASE.

SIMMONS IMMEDIATELY ROLLED THE BIG PHANTOM II HARD LEFT TO PURSUE.

PHWEEEEE

HERE WE GO!

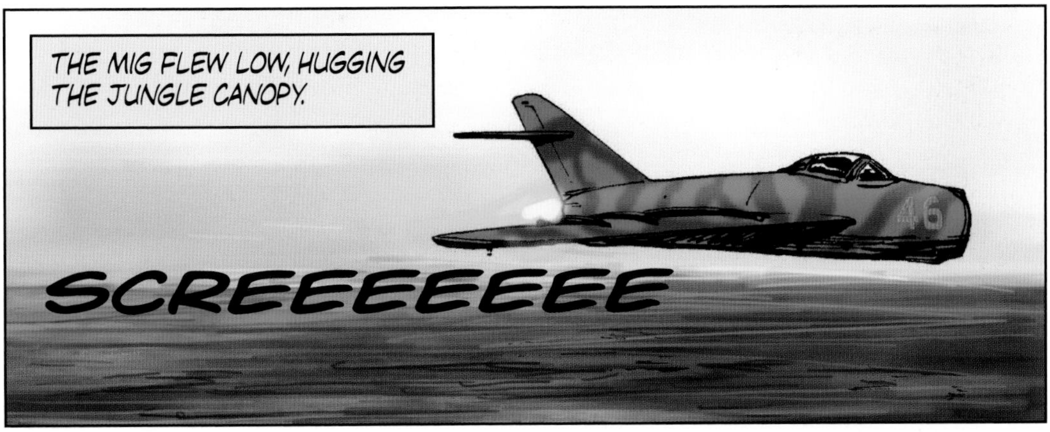
THE MIG FLEW LOW, HUGGING THE JUNGLE CANOPY.
SCREEEEEEEE

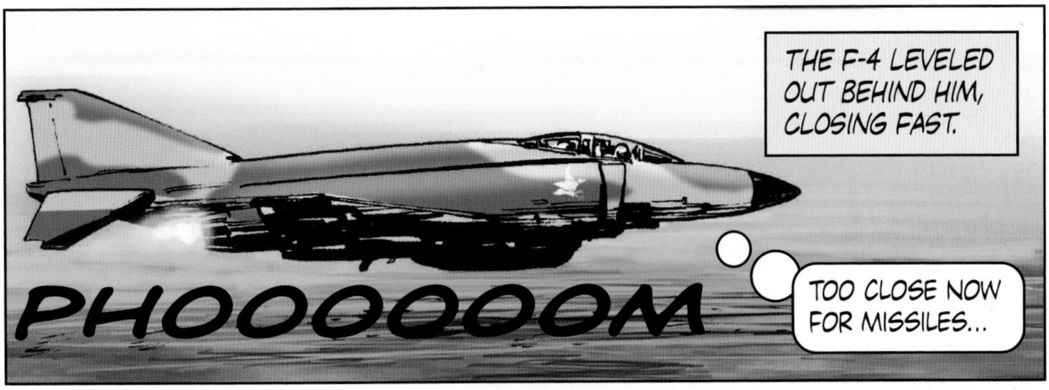
THE F-4 LEVELED OUT BEHIND HIM, CLOSING FAST.
PHOOOOOOM
TOO CLOSE NOW FOR MISSILES...

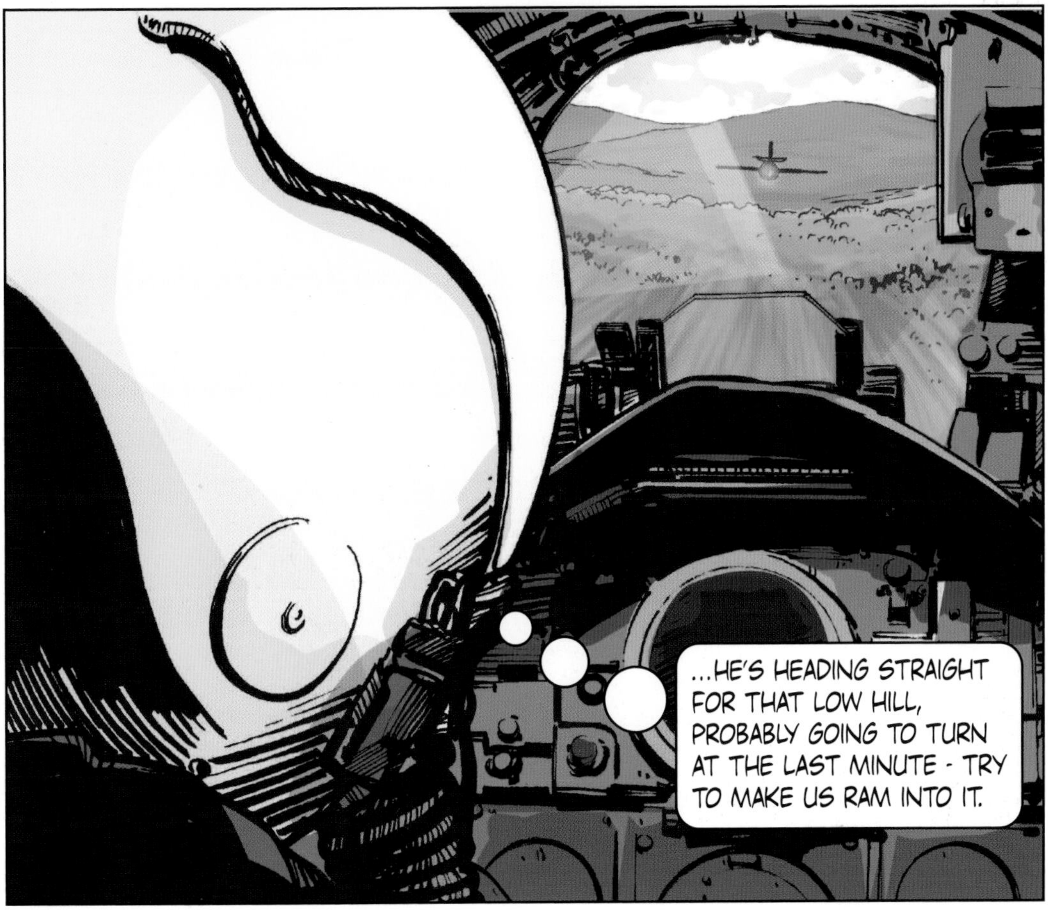
...HE'S HEADING STRAIGHT FOR THAT LOW HILL, PROBABLY GOING TO TURN AT THE LAST MINUTE - TRY TO MAKE US RAM INTO IT.

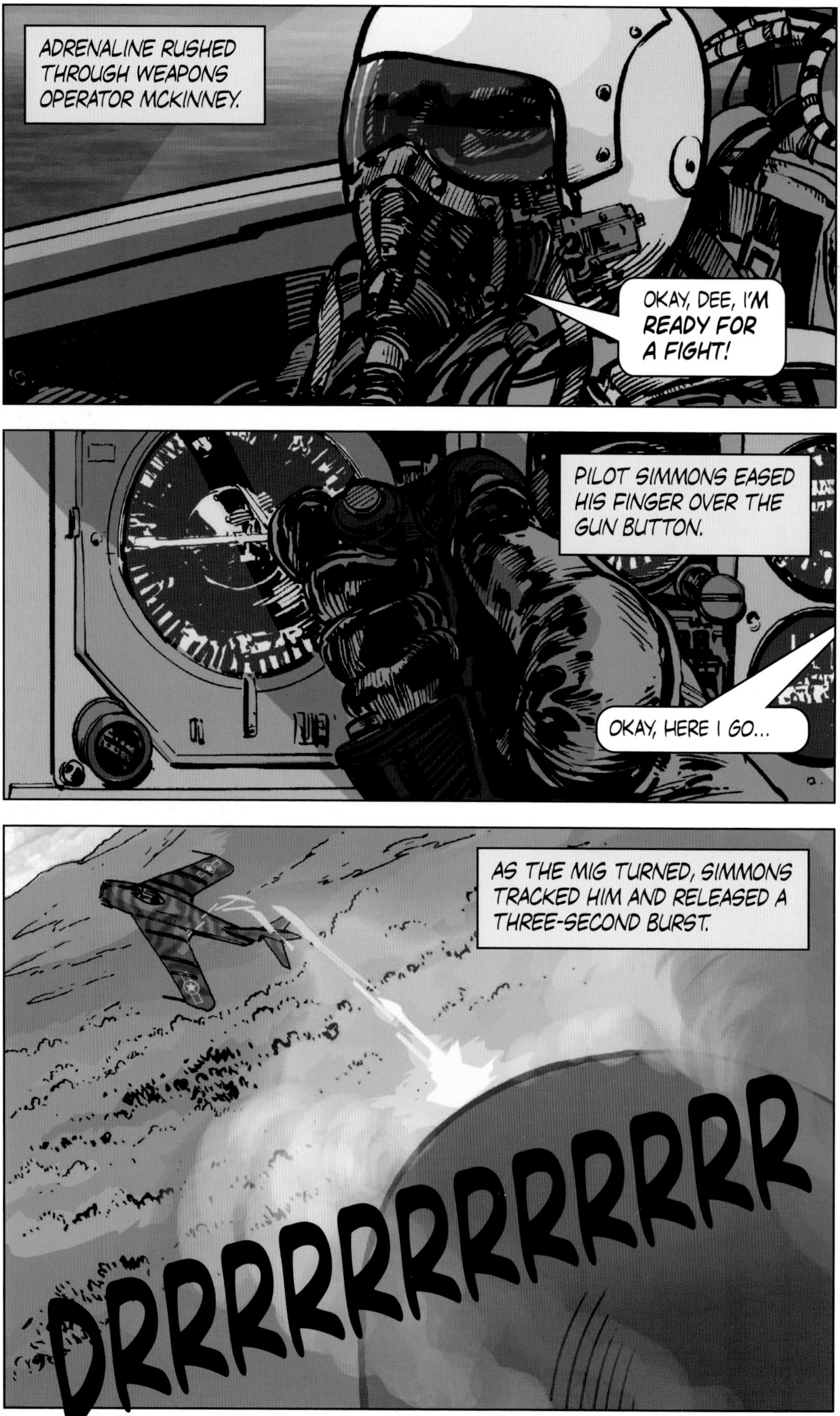
ADRENALINE RUSHED THROUGH WEAPONS OPERATOR MCKINNEY.
OKAY, DEE, I'M READY FOR A FIGHT!
PILOT SIMMONS EASED HIS FINGER OVER THE GUN BUTTON.
OKAY, HERE I GO...
AS THE MIG TURNED, SIMMONS TRACKED HIM AND RELEASED A THREE-SECOND BURST.
DRRRRRRRRRRRRR

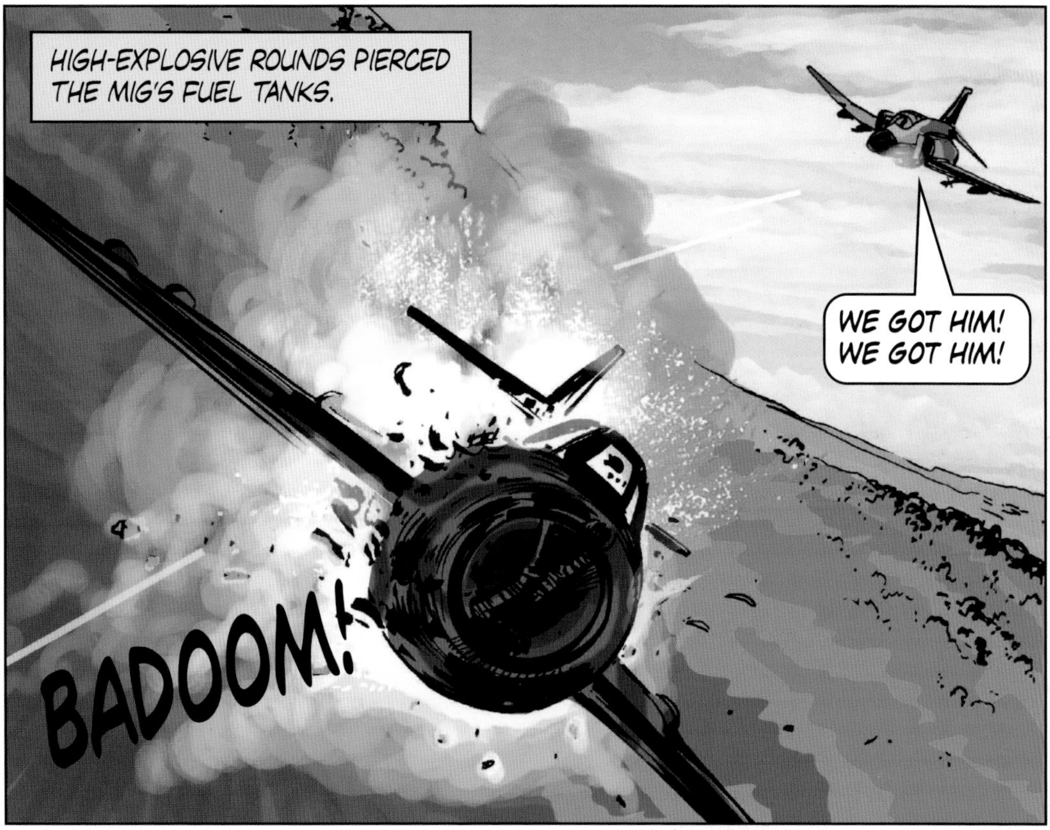
HIGH-EXPLOSIVE ROUNDS PIERCED THE MIG'S FUEL TANKS.
WE GOT HIM! WE GOT HIM!
BADOOM!

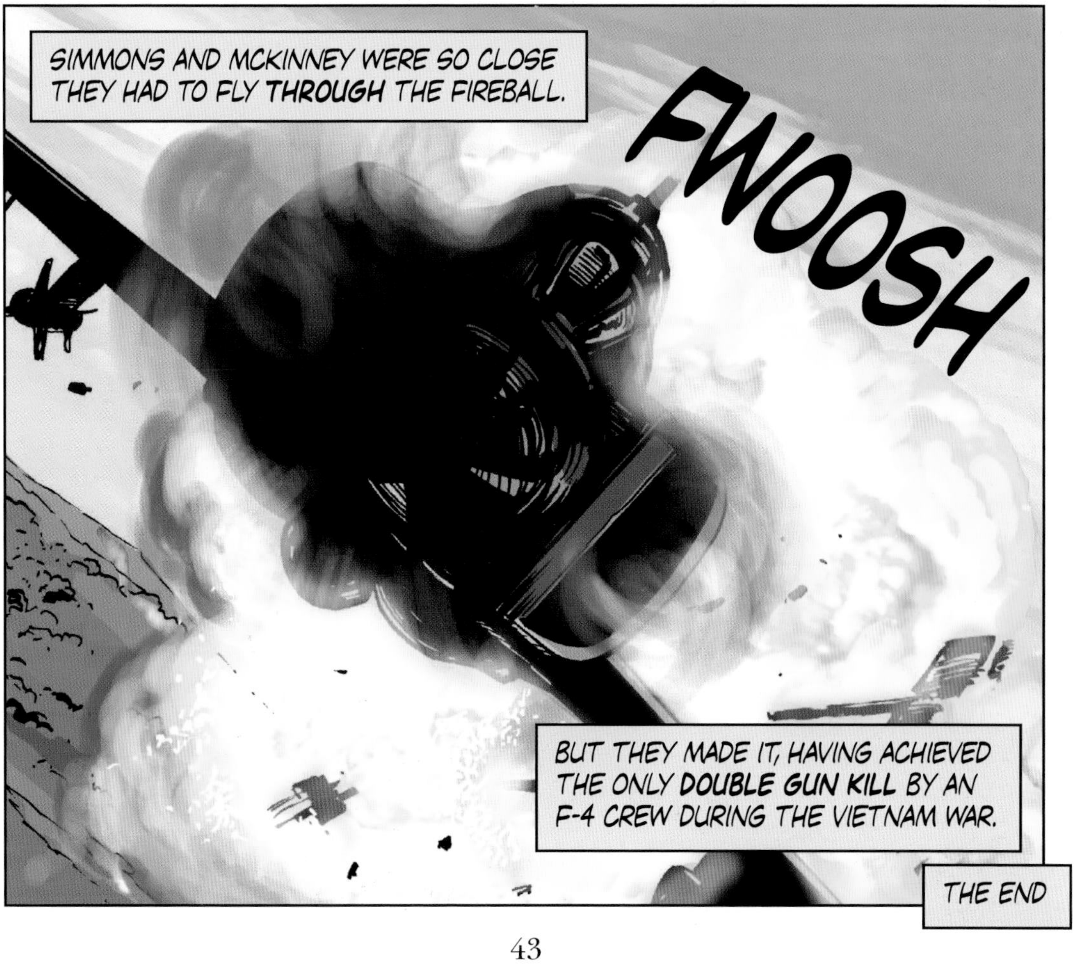
SIMMONS AND MCKINNEY WERE SO CLOSE THEY HAD TO FLY **THROUGH** THE FIREBALL.
FWOOSH
BUT THEY MADE IT, HAVING ACHIEVED THE ONLY **DOUBLE GUN KILL** BY AN F-4 CREW DURING THE VIETNAM WAR.
THE END

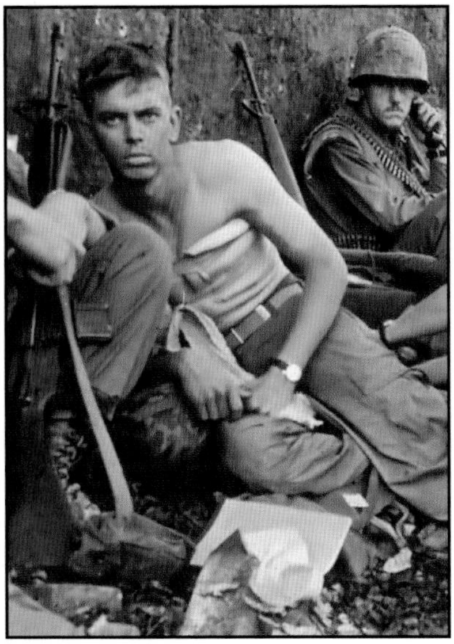

EXHAUSTION

During the Tet Offensive, 58,000 Viet Cong soldiers were killed, weakening their reign as a major force. Westmoreland requested a further 206,000 troops to pursue the survivors and possibly end the war.

Heavy casualties in each successive battle negatively impacted support for the war.

Endless War?

U.S. President Lyndon B. Johnson was caught in a bind. American troops in Vietnam had to be drafted. To send more troops in at that time would require calling up the National Guard. It would also mean committing the American economy to the war. Civil disobedience and protest in the country were at an all-time high, and no one could say when the war might end. Johnson refused the troops and announced he would not stand for re-election.

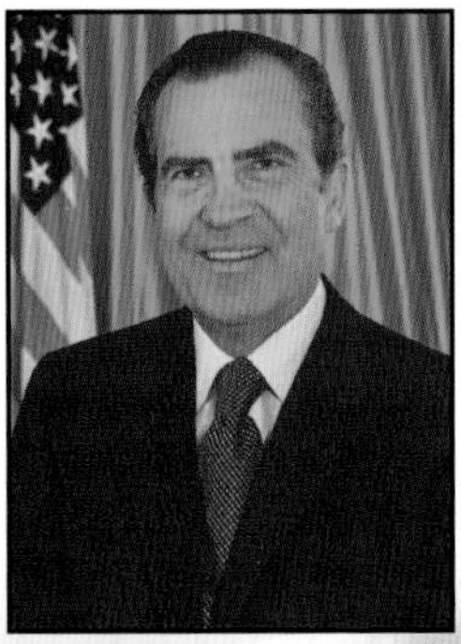

President Nixon was determined to find a way out of the war.

Aggressive Negotiations

The new U.S. president, Richard Nixon, authorized the steady withdrawal of American troops. He also gave the go ahead to bombing communist bases in Cambodia, which caused a wave of violent protests at home when it became public. An unsuccessful invasion of neighboring Laos by the South Vietnamese in 1971 led the North Vietnamese to make a limited invasion into South Vietnam in the spring of 1972. Meanwhile, Nixon tried to ease relations with China and negotiate for peace with Hanoi.

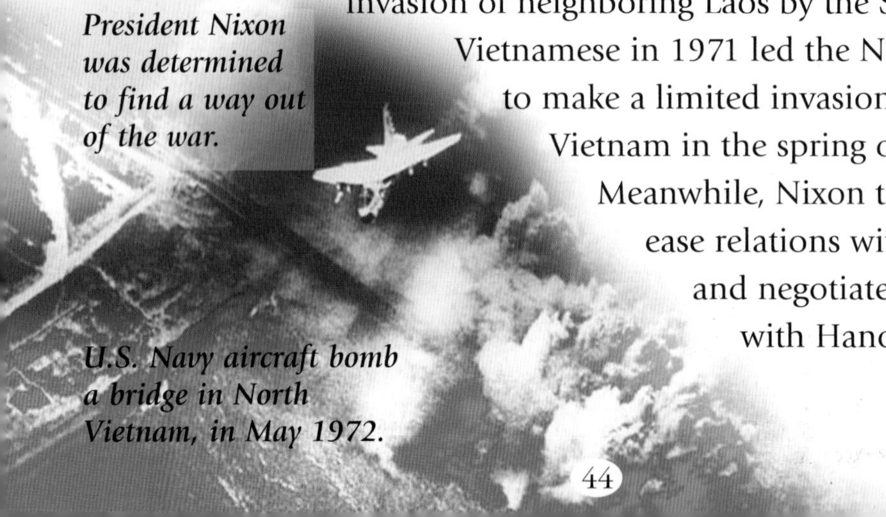

U.S. Navy aircraft bomb a bridge in North Vietnam, in May 1972.

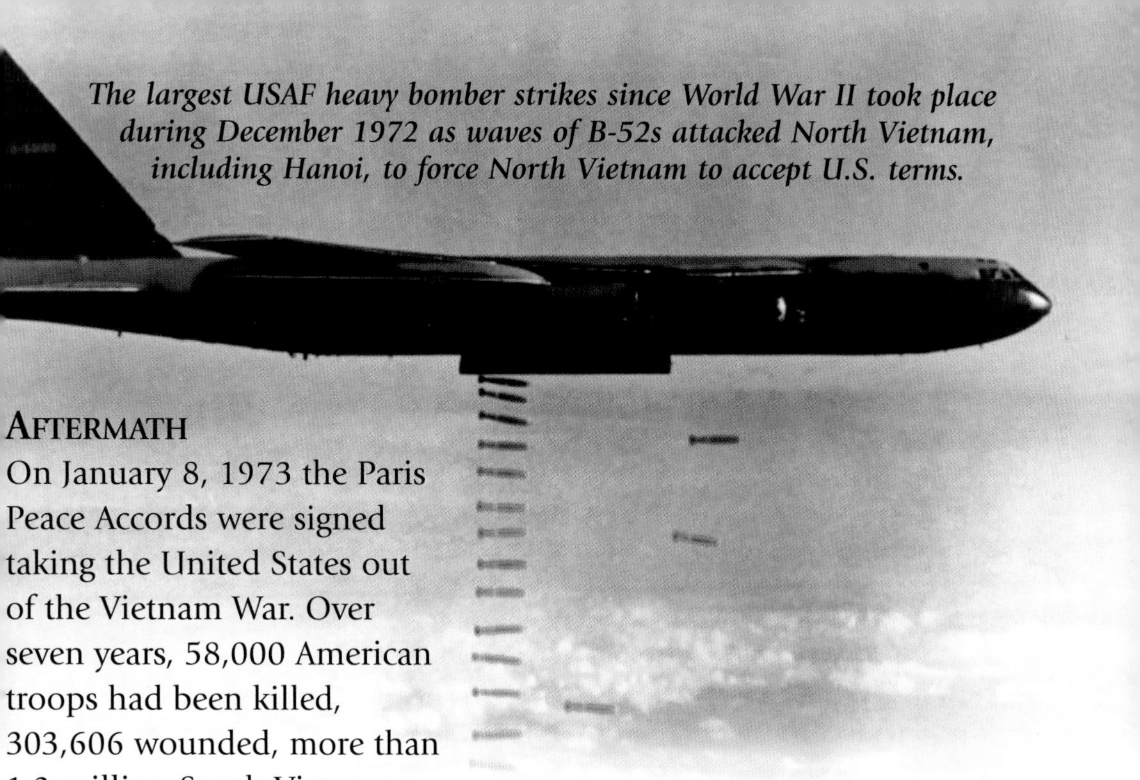

The largest USAF heavy bomber strikes since World War II took place during December 1972 as waves of B-52s attacked North Vietnam, including Hanoi, to force North Vietnam to accept U.S. terms.

Aftermath

On January 8, 1973 the Paris Peace Accords were signed taking the United States out of the Vietnam War. Over seven years, 58,000 American troops had been killed, 303,606 wounded, more than 1.3 million South Vietnamese troops were dead or wounded, and more than one million NVA/Viet Cong were killed, wounded, or missing. At least 250,000 civilians in North and South Vietnam also died. The war continued until North Vietnam overran Saigon, reuniting the country under communism in April 1975. In the late 1970s, 1.5 million Vietnamese "boat people," or refugees, fled Vietnam for the West.

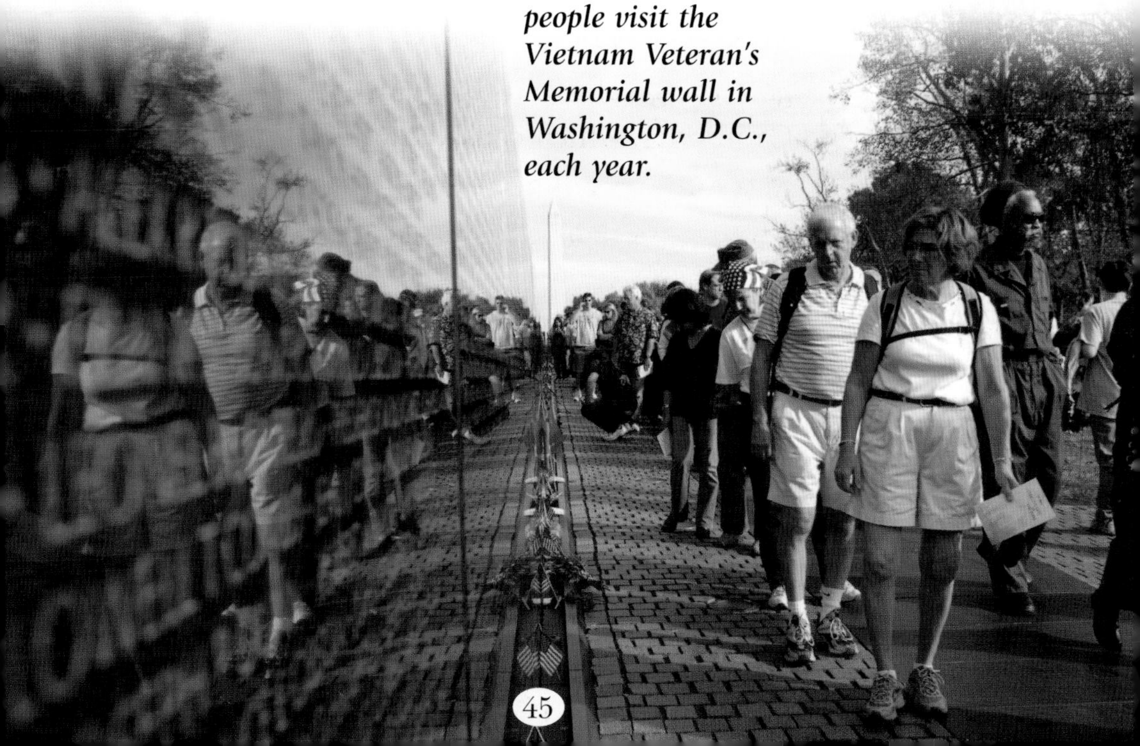

Two to three million people visit the Vietnam Veteran's Memorial wall in Washington, D.C., each year.

GLOSSARY

A-1 Skyraiders American single-seat attack aircraft

adrenaline A hormone released into the body when under stress

Agent Orange A poisonous chemical used by the U.S. military during the Vietnam War to strip forests of foliage to eliminate enemy cover

Allies The joint military forces fighting against Germany and Japan during World War II

ambush A sudden attack combined with the element of surprise

ammunition (ammo) Objects, such as bullets, that can be fired from guns

artillery High-caliber weapons used by crews during battle

back stick To pull back on an aircraft's control stick

boat people A term that usually refers to refugees from the Vietnam War who fled the country in small boats after the fall of Saigon

burners Refers to the afterburners on an aircraft which add thrust

canopy A transparent, weatherproof cover over an aircraft's cockpit; Also, the treetops of a forest

cease-fire A military order to stop attacks

charismatic Relating to a individual's personal charm or appeal

civil disobedience To refuse to obey a government's order, usually in a non-violent way, as a means of protest

civilians Citizens who are not fighting in the army

Cold War A period of political tension from 1947 to 1990 during which communist countries led by the Soviet Union and democratic countries from the West led by the United States competed militarily. Each side tried to control or influence unstable countries around the world in an effort to spread their own styles of government.

column A long line of troops

communist Someone who believes a political philosophy that says everyone should be treated equally and share all goods equally

corpsman Someone in the army trained to give minor medical aid

correspondent A journalist covering news from a foreign country

coups The overthrow of governments by groups determined to replace them with other bodies, either civil or military. A countercoup is an attempt by another group to overthrow the new government.

credibility Ability to inspire trust

decimated To be reduced drastically in number

deployment The movement of troops from one position to another

destabilized Caused an organization or government to be unable to operate as usual

domino theory A belief that when one country falls under the control of communism, countries that border it will follow

drafted When a citizen is selected for required national military service

escalation An increase in intensity

firefight A brief exchange of fire

Gs Units of force that gravity puts on a pilot's body during acceleration

guerrilla Relating to forces not part of the regular army

heat-seeking missile A weapon that aims itself toward jet engine emissions

ideologies Sets of beliefs that form the basis of political or economic systems

incendiary Capable of causing fire

infantry A unit of soldiers who fight on foot

medevac Medical evacuation

mortar A device used for throwing shells

napalm An extremely sticky jellied gasoline mixture used in bombs that sticks to skin and anything else it touches and which causes severe burns when set on fire

National Guard In the United States, a military force not on duty that can be called upon when regular army forces need to be supplemented

nationalists Members of a party who want independence for their country

occupation The control of an area or country by a foreign military

offensive A carefully planned military attack

parachute flares A flare used in military aircraft as a defense against heat-seeking missiles

pitch control A lever that changes the direction of the aircraft

radio ops Communication center in an army camp for radio operators

repressive Control by force of citizens' actions and free speech

rudder A part of a plane that helps correct direction and steer

small arms Handheld firearms

staging area A place where troops and equipment for a military mission are gathered together

tracer fire Chemical trails from ammunition that help shooters correct their aim

wingman A pilot whose aircraft is positioned behind and outside the leading aircraft in a formation

INDEX